7 Kids & 2 Ex-Wives!

How fixing "ME" fixed my Broken Family

Y.G. NYGHTSTORM

authorHOUSE®

AuthorHouse™
1663 Liberty Drive
Bloomington, IN 47403
www.authorhouse.com
Phone: 1-800-839-8640

First published by AuthorHouse   3/24/2010

ISBN: 978-1-4520-0246-0 (e)
ISBN: 978-1-4520-0245-3 (sc)

Printed in the United States of America
Bloomington, Indiana

This book is printed on acid-free paper.

DEDICATION

This book is dedicated to my son, Victor Sims, who was tragically taken away from us January 31, 2008. He was an awesome leader in the community and a MAN amongst men! My son would have wanted me to tell the unmitigated truth and show how the most awful events can bring about positive change and build strength to help others. I am so very proud of my son, and I hope when my life is over that he is just as proud of me. WE LOVE YOU VICTOR!

THE ROAD TO REDEMPTION

I SAT IN A run down, rat and roach infested motel room alone in a dark corner. Tears burned my eyes as the unmitigated truth slapped me across my face. My family was gone and it was all my fault! I wondered aloud, "How in the hell did it get this bad?" Is it really possible for a man with nothing but love in his heart to express himself so violently with his hands? I fought off the agony of another depressive cycle as I tried to justify the unthinkable.

The raw reality that I destroyed both of my marriages hurt me to the core. But what drove me to near suicide was the look on the faces of my seven young children. No longer did they see me as the hero, but as the vicious villain that hurt their mothers for no good reason other than a bruised ego.

The fact that I grew up in an abusive home, was raped by a mad man when I was a child, and was later diagnosed with severe Depression and Post Traumatic Stress Disorder was no excuse for my actions. The conversation I was having with myself was reasonable, it was normal to get upset when you are faced with unnecessary drama in your marriage, but still, I responded inappropriately! The sad thing was that no one cared what was done to me. All they saw was a large, intimidating black man scaring the sh*t out of a defenseless woman. This is a painful lesson that I will not repeat!

I prayed aloud to my Heavenly Father to forgive me. It seemed that God ignored me until I finally woke-up and took full responsibility for my foul actions. I was a good man that did some very bad things that I will forever be ashamed of. The only hope for my tortured soul was to change, not just to say I would but to do it. This change could not be a temporary quick fix; but a change that was to be rooted so deep in my spirit that not even my ex-wives could deny the new light that shone from me.

With the understanding that this task will be hard, and people would cruelly judge me; my purpose in this world could not be clearer. Allow God to change me and use me as a vessel to speak the TRUTH about the evils of domestic violence and how children in abusive homes may grow up to become abusers themselves. I will educate men who have lost their families, on how to fix what may seem to be impossible. But I first must fix "ME" and fix my own broken family. I did understand, however, that some people and situations could not be fixed. In these instances, for my own sanity, it would be best to distance myself from those who were not essentially vital to my having a relationship with my kids or the woman I wanted in my life.

Through positive change, hard work and the grace of God, I have done just that! I remarried my second ex-wife, mended the fence with my first ex-wife and took back my place as the HERO in the lives of my children! I learned how to change my life through my changed mind and actions, and so can you!

Y.G. Nyghtstorm

A PLEDGE TO MYSELF

STRONG PEOPLE MUST DO WHAT MUST BE DONE IN THE FACE OF ADVERSITY, FOR THEY KNOW THAT THEIR PAIN IS ONLY TEMPORARY.

I _____ agree to make the positive changes that I need to make to improve the lives of my children, others around me and, most importantly, myself. I understand that in order for change to come, I must take full responsibility of all of my actions, both good and bad. I believe that I can do or become whatever I want, and by the time I finish reading this book, I will be on my way to a much better life -- mentally, physically and financially.

Sign your name _____

Today's date _____

CONTENTS

MY STORY

Warning: I have more skeletons in my closet than stars in the sky! So get ready, set, here we go!

1.

THE PURPOSE IS BORN

"Fathers have unlimited power when they are operating and conducting themselves the right way."

I'M GOING TO USE George Lucas's (*Star Wars* creator) approach by starting in the middle of my story and working my way back to front. My life took a major turn when my youngest child was taken from me by the Department of Family and Children's Services (DFACS). I first want to say that there is a need for organizations like DFACS. There are so many cases of abuse and neglect against children in the United States that you wonder why some people bother to have kids at all. If you do not want children, then do not have them! They are not here for adults to manipulate, torture, and kill! It is unfortunate that an organization like DFACS has to exist.

One particular case was in New York where a crazed father named Juan Batista murdered his own two year old son in 2005. He hung his baby in a motel bathroom at the Crown Motor Inn in Queens because he was angry that the mother was dating someone else! This former personal trainer was a bodybuilder with a history of steroid abuse, failed relationships and suicide attempts actually thought that hurting the child would punish his ex. The police found the baby hanging by an extension cord from a shower curtain rod! This coward got 22 years to life in prison and had the entire community in a blood lust to see him fry for this heinous murder of his own child! The story was written by Herbert Lowe of Newsday.com March 21, 2005.

These types of fathers make it increasingly hard for all the good guys out here. They are the reason why the system does not trust us to be the primary care-givers to our kids in case of a divorce from the mother. Sure, there are plenty of cases in which the mother kills her children, such as Susan Smith (who pushed her car into a lake drowning her two children who were still in their car seats on October 25, 1994), and who can forget Andrea Yates (who drowned all five of her children in a bathtub June 20, 2001); however, in the all-seeing eyes of our society, women are not judged as harshly as men. This is an injustice that is prevalent, but it is slowly changing and will eventually correct itself. DFACS is a must to help stop monsters like this, but in my case, I feel that the actions of DFACS were a huge error that hurt my family to no end.

I remember that back in 2000, my second ex-wife, to whom I will refer as Deuce (wife #2), told me that she was pregnant over the phone, and I was so ecstatic that I ran around an entire apartment complex screaming that I was having another little girl. We both had two boys and a daughter from previous relationships, and we were excited because we would finally have a child together and create a stronger bond for the kids. This little girl would be everybody's baby sister, whether they were my kids or Deuce's. We went through the normal difficulties of pregnancy, and the baby was born at the end of the year.

We brought our beautiful baby girl home and everything was normal for a while. One day I noticed a bruise on the baby's leg while I was giving her a bath. She seemed to cry all the time when I touched her leg. Deuce and I were concerned so we took her to the hospital that night. Once we were there, the doctors ran x-rays and found a small hairline fracture on her leg. We were shocked and wondered how in the hell it happened. The doctor walked out and a DFACS worker walked in. She questioned us aggressively. We could not adequately answer her questions on how the baby was injured. I told the woman that I just discovered the injury, and I rushed her to the hospital. This was not good enough, and she told Deuce and me that she was taking custody of the baby! We were asked to leave, and she said she would be in touch in a few weeks with a court date!

Can you imagine someone literally taking your baby out of your arms without your having any say so at all, and then having the police escort you out of the hospital?! This was a grueling experience. Deuce could not compose herself as she cried uncontrollably. I had to help her walk out of the hospital as I cried as well. We were completely powerless, and it sickened us as we realized that the state literally has the power to kidnap your child whenever they feel like it!

We knew that getting her back would be the fight of our lives. We got home, rounded the children together, and told them what happened. The kids were devastated and told us that they would play with the baby and maybe they might have "play wrestled" with her too hard. Deuce and I knew that all the kids loved the baby and nothing malicious went on. This was an accident and nothing more! Knowing that we would have to fight to get our baby back, we contacted every attorney in the book, but they were all too expensive. We were struggling trying to take care of our children, and there was no money for an attorney. We tried to get a loan, but everyone turned us down. We sucked it up and took our chances with a public defender from the court. What a mistake that was!

We walked into the courtroom hoping for the best, but our so-called attorney was a poor excuse of a defender. He was practically on their side as he half-assed around and could barely speak. It was like he was afraid to challenge anything the state had to say. Deuce and I sat there as the state told the judge that we were awful parents and that the baby needed to be permanently taken away from us. We decided to stand up and speak for ourselves since Mr. Public Defender would not defend us! Deuce said that she strongly disagreed with the state's comments, and I added that the children simply played with the baby too roughly, and it was an accident. I took full responsibility for everything because I still should have monitored them better. The state was not satisfied and still pushed for our parental rights to be stripped! The judge delayed her judgment and decided to give us visitation rights every other weekend and set up another court date. This is not what we wanted, but we accepted it as a minor victory.

We were in and out of court for eleven months fighting to get our rights back. We even had the support of some DFACS workers who monitored us when we visited the baby. They were convinced that we were a loving family, and it truly was an accident. They noticed how much the baby cried as they took her out of my arms at the end of our visits. My little girl knew that I was her dad, and she did not want to leave me! I even cried as I gave her back knowing that there was a chance that my rights as her father could be taken away from me forever! It was possible that I might never see her again, and that just did not sit well with me! The DFACS workers took note and said that they would be there for me in court if they had to help me get her back. Uno (my first ex-wife) even stepped in, gave her support, and was willing to testify on my behalf if necessary. I appreciated the effort from her because we were not getting along too well at the time.

Armed with faith and the truth, Deuce and I went back to court determined to get our baby who was now one year old back. This hearing would determine if we would finally get her back for good or if she would be taken away from us forever to be raised by foster parents. Deuce and I held each other as we waited for our case to be called. Mr. Public Defender walked up to us and said that he did not know how it was going to go and that we needed to be prepared for the worst. The prosecutor would push for substantial jail time for us both. I told this simpleton that I would be speaking for us, and we no longer needed his so-called services. I fired his ass right there and did not blink as I stared him down! I was not going to risk the life of my baby in his hands! I took control of the situation and was determined to take on the state and not walk out of there without getting my child back!

Our case was called and we walked into the courtroom; the state attorney turned her nose up at us, but we ignored her. Deuce and I sat down, and the judge heard everything the state had to say to justify taking away our child. I was called up to the stand, and the judge asked me why she should grant us custody. I looked the judge in her eyes and told her that it was all my fault. I said that I was totally responsible for my baby getting hurt. In an effort to try to spend some alone time with

Deuce, I asked the kids to watch the baby. I explained that we did not have time for our relationship because we were always mom and dad. We needed just a little time to ourselves, and it was I who asked the kids to keep her entertained for an hour. I admitted that this was a mistake, and I see what can happen in a short time of no supervision and told the judge that I will never have such a lapse of judgment again.

I expressed how this tragedy had ripped a hole in my family and that we desperately wanted her back. This little girl should go home to be loved and cherished by her family instead of tolerated by some foster parents. I also told how I saw on the news some unfortunate events dealing with DFACS and some of the kids in the system. These kids were being abused and even killed by their foster parents! This was a future that I did not want for my baby and her place was with us where she would be loved. The state challenged everything I said and told the judge that those kids that were hurt or killed were just isolated incidents. I quickly stood up and shouted out *"Tell that crap to the parents of those kids who are dead and see what happens! This is unacceptable! You don't care at all about these kids! This is just a job to you, but this is our lives damn it!"* The judge told me to sit down and be quiet. I did as she instructed and tried to compose myself.

The judge thought long and hard. She admitted to seeing the stories on the news and was disturbed. The judge made her decision and spoke to the courtroom, *"We are supposed to be protecting children and helping families to mend if they have a desire to do so, not advocating the removal of a child from a loving household that made a mistake just to turn around and have the child hurt or killed while in our custody."* She looked at me sternly and told me to stand up. The judge told me that I had better pay close attention for now on and use proper judgment when dealing with my kids. She also said that the court would be monitoring me, but she saw no need to keep the baby from us any longer. She said to me, *"You're a good father sir, and make sure this never happens again."* "Yes ma'am!" I shouted. We got our baby back!

Deuce and I cried in the courtroom as the day that we had been praying for finally came! There are no words that can describe the feelings that we were experiencing at that time. All I know is that we looked that attorney for the state in the face and Deuce gave her a piece of her mind. *"Give her back, now. You should be ashamed of yourself."* Deuce said boldly. The attorney slammed our file on the table and shook her head. This woman was hellbent on taking our child from us. I spoke to her as well, *"We need people like you defending those kids that cannot defend themselves and saving them from parents who do not love them. Our child is not one of those kids. Its time she came home; now give her back."* She reluctantly responded, *"You will be reunited with your baby within the hour."*

This ordeal was a true test of faith and long-suffering, but we won! As a father, there will be times when you must take full responsibility and sometimes take matters within your own hands to fix them. I could not depend on that public defender to help us. The judge would not even listen to me until I took responsibility and convinced her that I would never let it happen again. I had to remember that I was the dad, and I was the ultimate authority in the household. That attorney tried her best to discredit me and permanently take away our baby, but she was powerless in the end. We never heard from the courts again and #7 is a beautiful, happy little girl surrounded with love.

Deuce and I lost everything in our battle to get our baby back, but we developed a bond that was not there before. We were happy for a few years until we both came to the conclusion that we were not compatible. We still loved each other, but we could not get it to work no matter how hard we tried. I was a good father, but I was an awful husband who had a lot of growing up to do. We agreed to go our separate ways and that I would have custody of #7. It is not easy to get a mother to part with her child by any means, but I convinced her that I could handle the duties of being a single dad.

I explained that she had the older three children (from her previous relationship); Uno had the younger three children (from my previous relationship) and I should at the very least contribute to the parent triangle by taking care of the baby full time. Deuce was worried because I had trouble remaining employed due to my severe depression. There were times when I could not show up for work due to my melancholy mood changes. She had good reason to be concerned, but she reluctantly agreed, and my journey into the unknown world of single parenting began. I could not afford to let her, my daughter, or myself down. I had a new job, and I was determined to keep it no matter what!

I started fresh and rented out a place that I paid weekly on, and Deuce sent the older three children (now teenagers) to live with their father and pursued her passion to be an over-the-road truck driver. I concentrated on building a homeless shelter for single fathers because it was something that I always wanted to do. I figured after fifteen years of procrastinating that this was the time to finally do it. I did not know at the time the urgent need of such a refuge for single dads, but I would soon find out.

I worked a typical nine-to-five during the day and concentrated on developing my business plan for the shelter at night. I worked this job to support me and the baby until the inevitable happened. I walked into the office one morning and I was informed that I was laid off! The company was going under, and they could not afford to pay me my last paycheck! I was kicked to the curb with no money and no way to pay rent because it was the first of the month! Sure, I could apply for unemployment but that takes weeks to kick in. I was finally able to get a job, keep the job, be very good at the job, fight off my depression for the job, and I still lost the job because of events beyond my control!

I was highly upset and threatened to burn down the establishment but that would have been unproductive. I collected myself and walked out with my head high. Despite the intentional shadowing of my emotions, I was scared and wondered how I was going to provide for my family. My child support was due to Uno and I still had a little baby at home to feed. I called a friend of mine that I have known since childhood who was a successful comic book artist, but he was out of town. I called all of my remaining friends but they were in financial jams themselves and could not help. *"I'll pray for you."* is all I heard as they hung up the phone. They couldn't help if they wanted to and the rental office put a little note on my door reminding me that the rent was late. Weekly places function differently from monthly places. If you do not pay rent, they can kick you out right then instead of filing an eviction notice to the county like most monthly rental properties.

I sweet talked my babysitter into watching #7, promising her that I would pay her when I got my check. I felt like garbage because I knew that I would not be able to pay her as I lied to her in her face. It was the middle of the summer, and I needed a place for the baby to go while I looked for work. I had every intention on paying her when I could, but the fact that I was facing eviction loomed over my head like a dark cloud. I pounded the pavement day by day, hitting all places that appeared to be hiring, including some temporary agencies, all with the same results. Employers were accepting applications but were not hiring at that time. I even applied at fast food places, but all the high school and college kids soaked those jobs up, so no flipping burgers for me. This was not helping my situation and time was running out.

I came home to my little one bed room apartment and found another note on the door. The office was more direct this time about putting us out within twenty-four hours if they did not receive the rent. I balled the notice up in my hand and tossed it aside as I opened the door to be greeted by my little girl and the babysitter. *"You're going to pay me aren't you?"* she asked in a concerned way. *"You know I got you girl."* I responded slowly. She knew at that point that I was not telling the truth because she knew my situation. She said nothing as she walked out of my apartment not bothering to close the door behind her. My daughter was looking at me with those big brown eyes wondering what was wrong with her daddy. I picked her up, sat on the couch, held my daughter and cried out of frustration because I would be homeless for the second time. I was homeless when I was eighteen years old, and I swore to myself that I would never go through that again, but apparently I was wrong. I'll get into that little adventure later (**chapter 7**).

The following morning, I began packing what little we had and loading it into my car. I called Deuce who was in Indiana learning how to drive tractor trailers and told her that I needed some money. I told her it was for a bill and not the rent. I did not want her to know that I was in this much trouble. I had given her my word that I would take care of our baby and not allow anything like this to happen. I was ashamed of myself for being in this situation, and I could not admit to her that I failed so soon after she was gone. She told me that she didn't have any money because she was still in training and not officially on the road. She questioned me further and asked what was wrong. I told her that all was well and hung up the phone telling yet another lie.

I finished packing up the car and put the baby in her car seat when apartment security walked from around the corner. They were coming to put me out and make sure I left the premises. I said nothing as I squeezed into my overly packed Geo and drove off. I felt that if worse came to worse, I could go to a family shelter for a while until I got back on my feet. I called a few of them, and they all told me that they were for WOMEN and children only! This upset me because they were saying that they were a "family" shelter and I have a "family" consisting of my daughter and myself, and they were rejecting us because I was a man! I heard this same song and dance everywhere I went. It amazed me that a city as big as Atlanta with so many resources had no place for a single man with a child.

There were plenty of homeless shelters for men, and I discovered that they were so run into the ground that it was not safe for me to be there, let alone my daughter. These places shot me down quickly when they saw my baby because they were afraid that she may be molested by someone, and they could not afford a potential law suit. The most ridiculous item of the day was when I called the last shelter and this lady (using the term loosely) told me to turn my daughter over to DFACS until I got on my feet, and they would let me stay there.

I was appalled at the very statement that I would have to relinquish custody of my child to the state in order for the state to help me simply because I was a man! I had fought with DFACS for my daughter, and there was no way in hell that I would just give her back to them! I told this woman that it was not fair that single mothers get so much help from everywhere, and they are never told to give up their kids for assistance, but a man is treated differently. She so eloquently replied, *"Then build your own damn shelter!"* as she slammed down the phone.

That is when I realized how important it was to finish what I had been planning and create a place for fathers like myself to go when they need help. All of this enlightenment was fine and dandy, but my daughter was getting tired, and I needed a place for us to go. I flipped through a Creative Loafing paper and saw some rooms for rent for just $100 a week. I made one last call to the comic book artist again, and he picked up the phone. I asked to borrow the hundred bucks, and he said yes without asking what I needed it for! I got the room, landed a job and busted my butt to never get in that position again!

I learned from that experience that all things happen for a reason. I was a good employee on this particular job, but I was still laid off for reasons beyond my control. Bad things happen to good people all the time for no apparent reason, but we must adjust and figure out the lesson later. I needed to go through these experiences to give me a solid purpose to push me to build a place for single fathers. I'm still working on this project and hopefully it will come to fruition because there are too many good men out there who need help.

Men should never have to give up their children for assistance! Will Smith portrayed **Chris Gardner** in the movie *The Pursuit of Happyness* dealing with the subject, but I actually lived it years before the movie's release, and I desperately want this problem solved! I want to remind everyone reading this book that *fathers have unlimited power when they are operating and conducting themselves the right way.*

I will say this again; you have the power because you are the dad. Universal circumstances tried to force me back into homelessness and destitution, but they failed! The state of Georgia tried to permanently take away my daughter, and it failed too! To all the good dads out there, always remember that nothing can stop you, not even the state. All I have to do now is invent a way to permanently cure severe depression and PTSD. I could take the billions of dollars I would earn from the landmark discovery and build housing for all single parents around the country. But since that has not happened yet, I guess you have to keep reading, and I'll keep trying!

7 Kids Challenge #1: Is there an issue that you have been putting off that needs your attention? Only YOU can solve YOUR problems so stop wasting time. Procrastination kills success! I challenge you to put this book down and handle your business of what you clearly know you NEED to be doing right now. I'll be here when you get back.

2.

MISERY LOVES CHAOS AND
THE ABSENTEE DAD

*"When there is no direction or purpose,
chaos will lead and destruction follows."*

PEOPLE ALWAYS ASK ME what my definition of the word father is. I always respond with just one word, LEADER. The purpose of every father is to provide leadership and structure to his children in an ever-growing, chaotic world. I have a ton of experience with this subject because I spent so much time being sick with depression that my kids were suffering. Everything corrected itself when I got right and handled the very important job of being a hands-on dad. Unfortunately, many fathers have elected to pursue wealth and women as opposed to dedicating their lives to their children.

The term "fatherless" has been a widespread word that has dug its ugly claws into all societies and races of people across the planet. The overwhelming problems that are attached with this word are extremely disturbing! Studies have shown that neighborhoods consisting of fatherless homes tend to be prone to higher rates of crime. In 1995, U.S Senator Phil Gramm made a comment referring to young boys growing up without fathers. The senator said, *"The odds that a boy born in America in 1974 will be murdered are higher than the odds that a serviceman in World War II would be killed in combat."* I found that shocking because I was born in 1974!

The connection between fatherless homes and out of control teens can not be ignored and swept under the rug anymore. This is a serious problem that is affecting us all in more ways than one. Too many men with indolent efforts, at best, believe that being a dad is just not important enough to garner their attention and, therefore, have abandoned their children to grow up in a tumultuous world. From 1968 to the present is a period that I call the "Bleeding Out Cycle." It seems that throughout all cultures, there was a gradual decline in the father's place in the home. Some so-called experts say that this was just a huge problem in the black community, but I strongly disagree! This is not a race issue but a societal issue that is spreading like a cancer killing families from within.

With the popularization of more illegal street drugs and the urge to chase scandalous women around or so-called "pimping," the attention of a lot of men in the United States shifted from family and commitment to the pursuit of pleasure. There was a great push in the social order of things as well. With the Vietnam War and racism ripping the country apart, it seemed that these frivolous pleasures uplifted many men who felt thrown away by society in one way or the other. You may still be wondering how this connects with fatherhood. Well look at it like this. When an individual is experiencing negativity in life, most want a quick fix to feel good.

Many men overindulge in pleasure to suppress the pain that they are feeling because they were not properly trained to deal with their emotions. Nine times out of ten, these indulgences have negative characteristics that tend to do more harm than good (drug abuse, alcoholism, promiscuous activities, high risk behavior, etc). The testosterone-driven man does not care about the harm that he is inflicting on himself and simply wants to stop the feelings of rejection by fulfilling the desire to be loved and accepted by his peers. He does not care how this "faux delight" comes about, even though it may be detrimental to him. He just wants the pain to go away! He wants to feel like he has some control over his life and that he possesses some semblance of power through the dominance of other men and especially women.

Men have a tendency to look around and focus on all the things that they do not have and look at the guy with the fancy car, all the money and all the women. We as men are not that complicated. Money, power and women are our biggest motivators! More money leads to more power; more power provides more opportunities to sleep with more exotic and extravagant women. In the midst of all of this may come some undesired children from some of these chicks that you never want to see again! I dare to be real with this subject because you just wanted to "hit it" and be done, but now you have a life-long attachment with her and you regret ever meeting her in the first place! This perpetuates the "fatherless" cycle!

This is going to hit some of you hard. Situations like these are never easy to fix and normally end with another rejected child who grows up and does the same thing allowing the cycle to never end. Maybe you were one of these thrown away fatherless kids, and you are pissed at your dad for leaving you because he could not deal with your mom. *Children follow the lead of their fathers, so where are you leading them?*

One of the main laws of the universe is that **when there is no direction or purpose, chaos will lead and destruction follows.** The biggest example I have of this rule is the once mighty and great Roman Empire. If you know your history, you know just how powerful and influential this culture was. There are signs of this culture all around us through architecture, entertainment and even our way of governing. Surely, such an empire as powerful and wise as Rome would survive forever, right? WRONG! They crashed and burned for a single reason, CHAOS!

Rome's destruction came from chaotic inner cores that led to weakened defenses and ultimate destruction. THERE WAS NO LEADERSHIP! All the great leaders of the past like Julius Caesar were long dead. Fathers were too concerned with seeking power and wealth rather than the welfare of their families. Most men were killed in battles leaving nothing but fatherless homes in their wake.

I mentioned earlier that neighborhoods consisting of mainly fatherless homes have a dramatic influx of crime. Rome was no different than any city in the modern United States. Crime rates rose to an astronomical level resulting in a high number of murders in the city. Fathers were not home to protect their families and to lead the misguided youths that were committing the majority of the crimes. Does this stuff sound familiar? Eventually, Rome became overrun with chaos and the outside barbarians saw a weak city ripe for the picking. Ask yourself this question: Does your home resemble Rome?

Father = Leader

As I said earlier, the word father means leader. If you look the word leader up in the dictionary, it says, "somebody who guides or directs others by showing them the way or telling them how to behave." This sounds like a father to me! The family unit is structured much like a human body. Each body part has a special job to preserve life. Fathers are the head of the family. Without the head, there will be no life! Think about that for a moment. I cannot stress enough how important your role is to your children. What are the qualities of a leader?

1. *Strength*
2. *Selflessness*
3. *Patience*
4. *Commitment*
5. *Understanding*
6. *Empathy*
7. *Wisdom*
8. *Diligence*
9. *Caring*
10. *Trustworthy*

Do any of these qualities apply to you? I hope that by the time you finish reading the book they all will. Remember one of the words is *patience*. It took me a long time to get this right. I do not expect you to get it immediately. In order to be a good father and leader, it takes lots of time and training. Most of us were never trained by our dads, so we had to wing it. Well, those days are over. We've made our mistakes, and now it is time to do it right. Now let's break these qualities down.

1. STRENGTH *noun*

Synonyms – power, force, might, potency, vigor

Definition - The physical or mental power that makes somebody or something strong.

+ My experience: Being the product of a divorced home takes strength. Surviving two divorces takes a lot of strength! Finding myself and realizing that I am not the scum of the Earth because I could not make it work with my ex-wives (regardless of what negative things their families said about me) took strength. Above all, overcoming the fact that they had moved on with their lives with other men took a great deal of emotional strength. That really hurt and took a long time to get over! I am sure you understand.

Write down an example of when you showed strength in your life.

Write down an example of when you needed someone to show you strength.

2. SELFLESSNESS *noun*

Synonyms – unselfishness, self-sacrifice, altruism

Definition - Putting other people's needs first.

+ My experience: Having seven children it seems that everyone's needs came before mine. I remember when I wanted to buy a nice sports car. It was the right color, had beautiful custom wheels, and the car lot was going to cut me a great deal! Then there was the minivan parked outback. The fact that I had seven kids made the decision for me. The needs of the family outweighed my want for the car. I bought the minivan okay! If that is not selfless, I do not know what is!

Write down an example of when you showed selflessness in your life.

Write down an example of when you needed someone to show you selflessness.

3.   PATIENCE *noun*

Synonyms – endurance, staying power, tolerance, lack of complaint, persistence, fortitude, serenity.

Definition - The ability to endure waiting or delay without becoming annoyed or upset or to persevere calmly when faced with difficulties.

- ✦ My experience: In chapter one, I described an awful moment in my life when my youngest daughter was taken away from the family by child protective services. In case you're skipping around the book and not reading it in order, I'll briefly catch you up. She had accidentally gotten hurt in the house. Her mother and I were devastated because they took our baby away for an entire year over an accident! We had to go to court and constantly fight to get our child back! This was a grueling experience but a fight that I refused to lose! To make a long story short, we got her back! This incident burned a hole in my heart but through patience, I won the battle!

Write down an example of when you showed patience in your life.
Write down an example of when you needed someone to show you patience.

4.   COMMITMENT *noun*

Synonyms – promise, pledge, vow, obligation, assurance, binder, dedication, loyalty

Definition - Something that takes up time or energy, especially an obligation. Devotion or dedication, for example, to a cause, person or relationship. A planned arrangement or activity that cannot be avoided.

+ My experience: There is nothing like being in a committed relationship in which your partner is not as committed as you are. This was a point in my life at which I really had to evaluate whether I really wanted to be with this woman. I was faithful, but she kept finding ways to constantly do the wrong thing. I felt like I had lost my soul. This experience showed me that commitments are not always returned to you as you give them, but her character was ruined, not mine. Even though I did not get out of the relationship the things that I needed at the time, I stayed true. She finally came around and became one of the best girlfriends I ever had. We are still very good friends today.

Write down an example of when you showed commitment in your life.

Write down an example of when you needed someone to show you commitment.

5.   UNDERSTANDING *noun*

Synonyms – sympathetic, considerate, thoughtful, kind, accepting, indulgent, perceptive, appreciative

Definition - The ability to perceive and explain the meaning or the nature of somebody or something.

+ My experience: My middle daughter (a preteen at the time) had a crush on one of my mom's co-workers. We thought it was quite innocent until her mother found a secret letter that she had written about the man. Let's just say that my daughter's imagination about sex and love was a little more advanced than I had thought! The guy had no idea of the crush, so I didn't go after him. I sat my little princess down and had "The Talk" with her. I told her about true love and added that sex with a grown man is never appropriate for a child. I had to understand that she was growing up and her hormones were starting to kick in. It was just one of those crushes that all little girls have. As long as it remained just a crush, I was cool with that. Lord knows I dreamed about Janet Jackson and Vanessa Williams as a kid with a ton of playboys under the bed!

Write down an example of when you showed understanding in your life. Write down an example of when you needed someone to show you understanding.

6.   EMPATHY *noun*

Synonyms – sympathetic, compassionate, considerate, feeling, concerned, kindhearted

Definition - The ability to identify with and understand another person's feelings or difficulties.

- ◆ My experience: My oldest son's girlfriend came over looking for him one day. I told her that he was not home but noticed the tear tracks running down her face. I brought her in and asked her what was wrong. She had just had a huge fight with her dad, and he had kicked her out. She could not understand why he was so protective over her and did not want her to date anyone. I felt empathy for her because I remember the huge fights my mother and I would get into. I also identified with her dad. I told her concisely that her dad loved her and that sometimes I did the same things with my kids. I even warned my son about her and told him that he needed to focus more on his books instead of a relationship. She understood. After another hour of spewing her guts to me and crying out about a hundred tissues, she went home and made peace with her dad.

Write down an example of when you showed empathy in your life.

Write down an example of when you needed someone to show you empathy.

7.   WISDOM *noun*

Synonyms – understanding, knowledge, insight, perception, astuteness, intelligence, acumen, good judgment.

Definition – The knowledge and experience needed to make sensible decisions and judgments, or the good sense shown by the decisions and judgments made.

+   My experience: This is something that happened years ago. I was in a great relationship with this wonderful woman. I had to go out of town on business for a few days. I wrapped things up early and return home only to find the "wonderful" love of my life in my bed with another man! Two things went through my mind. Kill this guy, and kill this guy! The anger surged through my veins, and since I am a big guy, I could have snapped him in two very easily. Weird as it sounds, I heard a voice in my head say, *"Do not destroy your life over someone who will not live for you."* It freaked me out at first, but I made the decision not to attack. I walked away from the situation and the relationship. Years later, I ran into her, and she had three kids by the guy, and he had left her high and dry. She told me that she regretted cheating on me and that he had given her herpes because of cheating on her! True wisdom knows that *what goes around comes around. You never have to punish anyone because the universe will do it for you!* Hahahahaha!!!!!

Write down an example of when you showed wisdom in your life.

Write down an example of when you needed someone to show you wisdom.

8.   DILIGENCE *noun*

Synonyms – meticulous, conscientious, thorough, attentive

Definition – Persistent and hard-working effort in doing something.

+ My experience: A true act of diligence was when I was talking to my oldest son about graduating from high school. He had already been kept back a grade in school, and he was continuing to slack off. Hanging out with his friends and playing basketball were more important to him than his education. He always said that he wanted nice things and to become a firefighter. I told him that he would never achieve these things without hard work and an education. This was a sort of mental war between us for years. Every time he brought home his report card, I pointed at all the bad grades and reminded him of what "he" said that "he" wanted to do, and there was no chance in hell of his achieving those goals. I used a little reverse psychology, and after a little while, I noticed a change within him. When he turned eighteen, his grades gradually improved. All the talks that I had with him finally clicked. He realized that he was now a man, and he needed to handle his business. He graduated high school and made me proud!

Write down an example of when you showed diligence in your life.

Write down an example of when you needed someone to show you diligence.

9. CARING *adjective*

Synonyms – kind, thoughtful, gentle, helpful, considerate, compassionate, concerned, loving

Definition – Compassionate or showing concern for others.

- ✦ My experience: My youngest son, whom everyone calls "The Terror," was misbehaving in school again. His mother (Uno) had called me, told me that she was frustrated with him, and wanted me to step in. Let's just say that I frequented his school a lot over the years. It seemed that he calmed down for a while when I showed up and went back to mischief when I left. This was quite taxing on the teachers and his mom. Instead of beating the boy, I sat my son down and asked him what the problem was. He looked into my eyes and said *"Daddy I want you."* He felt left out and unloved because his mother and I divorced soon after he was born. I had to hold my son and reassure him of my love for him and his place in my heart. I will go more into this particular story later (*chapter 7*).

Write down an example of when you showed caring in your life.

Write down an example of when you needed someone to show you caring.

10. TRUSTWORTHY *adjective*

Synonyms – dependable, reliable, responsible, truthful, honest, constant, honorable, upright

Definition – Deserving trust, or able to be trusted.

- ✦ My experience: My oldest daughter had gotten a new boyfriend. Things were getting serious between the two of them. Naturally, I was concerned for her welfare and feelings. I wanted to talk to her about it, but she always shut me out. She was afraid to talk to me because I would always fly off the handle when it came to her dating. Well, let's just say that I had to change my ways in a hurry! Her mother (Deuce) was out of town, and she really needed to talk. I sat her down and told her that I loved her very much and that I respected her enough to listen without judgment. I gained her trust at that moment, and we had a nice talk. I learned that *to get your kids' attention, you first have to listen* to them; then the trust will come.

I want to add finally, yet importantly, my son who bears my name. He is such a great kid and so trustworthy that I do not have any issues with him. He is the quiet one or maybe just smart enough to fly under my radar while everyone else gets in trouble! I'm watching you kid! Eventually, I will find something on you! Until then, keep up the good work! *Write down an example of when you showed that you were trustworthy.* *Write down an example of when you needed someone to be trustworthy.*

To lead means being the first one in the battle and working along side your troops as opposed to just dictating. The reason for this exercise is that you needed to see that *true leadership precedes results*. You wrote down examples of your doing positive things before you wrote down examples of when you needed someone to do the same thing for you. *If you need something in your life, provide that need for someone else first.* I hope that you are really paying attention. Doing this can be hard sometimes, but it works! Not being there for your kids the way you should will bring nothing but chaos to them. Thank you for stepping up because being a dad may be the fight of your life. I did not say being the leader would be easy.

Cup Cake Daddies

There are plenty of dads who continue to be there for their children, even though they do not live at home, and I will constantly praise them for their dedication and efforts, but there are cases when the father is home and the child is still fatherless. These dads are pushovers and are at home physically but choose to let their wives be the primary caregivers to the children. I call these men *"Cup Cake Daddies"* because of their sorry, pitiful lack of enforcement in the house while not supporting the mother!

I saw a television program in which a European nanny goes to different American family homes to help the parents with their out-of-control children. This nanny went into a home where the small children (5 years old and 3 years old) were terrorizing the mother and sometimes striking her when she did not give them candy. Dear old dad was stretched out on the couch reading a magazine while all of this drama was happening right in front of him! The sorry bastard did nothing as his pint sized brats whaled away on their mother! She screamed in frustration while looking at the so-called "man" of the house.

These children did not respect their mother in the least because Dad failed to lay down the law. He allowed chaos to rear its ugly head in his house, and he did nothing! It took an over- the- hill prune of a nanny from London to enforce the rules in his house and tell his kids that it was never okay to hit their mom. The nanny showed on national television that she had bigger balls than the dad, and he should have been ashamed of himself!

For all those absentee dads out there, I hope that you realize chaos cannot help but consume your kids like the "Cup Cake Daddy's" family. They need you! Structure and order can be implemented from outside the home. As long as they know that dad is watching, most children tend to stay out of trouble. Fathers are more than just a paycheck and are vital to the welfare of their children.

David Popenoe wrote an excellent book dealing with this issue. In his book *Life Without Father*, he talks about fatherless homes from a child's point of view. *"Obviously, children prefer to have a father in the home!"* Through empirical studies, Popenoe identifies many of the outcomes of fatherless homes, including juvenile delinquency, depression, substance abuse, and violence. A U.S. longitudinal study by **Cynthia Harper** and **Sara S. McLanahan** called *Father Absence and Youth Incarceration* tracked over 6,400 young boys over a period of twenty years and found that children without their biological fathers in the home were roughly three times more likely to be incarcerated. Another study by **Diana E. H. Russell** (*The Prevalence and Seriousness of Incestuous Abuse: Stepfathers vs. Biological Fathers*) showed that the rate of sexual abuse of girls by their stepfathers has a 40% greater chance of happening than sexual abuse by their biological fathers who remain in intact families. Study these statistics, and see if your kids fall in any of these categories.

1. US Dept. Of Health/Census - 63% of children committing suicide are from fatherless homes and 90% of all homeless and runaway children are from fatherless homes.

2. U.S. Dept. of Justice - 70% of youths incarcerated come from fatherless homes.

3. National Principals Association Report - 71% of all high school dropouts come from fatherless homes.

4. Criminal Justice & Behavior, Volume 14, p. 403-26 - 80% of rapists come from fatherless homes.

5. Center for Disease Control - 85% of all children who show behavior disorders come from fatherless homes.

6. Fulton Co. Georgia, Dept. of Correction - 85% of all youths in prison come from fatherless homes.

How important are you Dad? Is this happening to your child?

I looked at these statistics, and my mouth hit the floor because of the dramatic increase of homeless teens, teen suicide, teens with behavioral disorders and so on. What is really disturbing is that 80% of rapists grew up in homes without a father! These statistics show the increasingly negative impact on society when fathers are not there for their children. This is true chaos!

It is painfully obvious that you are extremely important regarding the well being of your children. I also found in my research and sometimes in my own experience that angry mothers play a pivotal role in sabotaging a father's visitation with his kids and even attempting to turn the kids against their dad because of the divorce or end of the relationship. Please do whatever you can to mend fences with your ex, and be there for your children. I had to do this for years before the drama ceased with my two ex-wives, but the walls of hate, deep hurt and unforgiveness gradually fell over time. I'll go into my screw-ups and all of that drama with my exes later.

To all of those who have an ex-wife from hell or "baby momma drama," seek immediate counsel from an attorney, and fight for your rights! Be prepared to spend a small fortune because the deck is stacked against you simply because you are a man! The system is designed to protect women, and it will aggressively make sure that she has the upper hand in court unless you can prove that she is an unfit parent. It seems wrong to me that you have to assassinate your ex-wife's character in order to make things "fair" for you in court! Unfortunately, that's the way it is until the judicial system stops seeing women as weak and incapable of taking care of themselves. No good can ever come from destroying her in court because somehow you will end up looking like the bad guy. You're screwed if you do, and you're screwed if you don't! All you can do is fight for your rights, be as fair as you can, and let your attorney do all the talking!

7 Kids Challenge #2: Are you a Cup Cake Daddy? I challenge all Cup Cake Daddies to immediately apologize to their spouses and responsibly enforce the rules in the house that the parents must be respected at all times. Your wife will LOVE you for this!

3.

WHY THE "GOOD MAN" GETS CHEATED ON!

"…even if I feel that someone is wrong, I need to make the proper decision that will lead to a positive conclusion."

THIS IS FOR ALL the single dads! Now that you are a single father, guess what? You have no time to cry over a failed relationship! Things happen that are beyond your control, and you have to pick up the pieces of your life and move on. I understand that society says that a man's feelings are totally irrelevant in a relationship. I honestly remember going to counseling with one of my ex-wives, and the therapist emphasized how I needed to be more aware of her feelings and understand that sometimes a woman needs to do things that a man may not understand. It sounded like total crap to me because I explained that she was cheating!

My wife had no excuse for her behavior, and I did not need to understand a thing! It seemed that this therapist gave all her female clients

33

a "poor woman" excuse. She constantly said that sometimes women just have to do things to make them feel better. These things can be positive and negative. I think that is the biggest crock that I have ever heard!

I look at relationships in one way. Treat your lover the way you want to be treated. It is the golden rule of the universe. I hear all the time from women that they are dating a "no-good" man. One of my female friends was telling me about a guy she had been dating for a while. She said that he was a bad boy that looked like Brad Pitt and that excited her. He had four children by four different women. He always told her that these women were giving him a hard time about child support. She even started helping him pay the child support. One day she took a pregnancy test and discovered that she was pregnant. She called her boyfriend over and told him. He immediately told her that he needed some space and that they needed to slow down the pace of their relationship. She was quite furious as he denied the child and said that he was not the daddy!

She later called a friend of hers to tell her about the "no-good" man. The friend regretfully informed her that she was sleeping with the same guy and had been doing so behind her back for months! The moral of the story is that this woman wanted a bad boy and that is what she got, a bad boy. I told her not to get mad because she brought all of that drama on herself. She knew how he was in the beginning.

Unfortunately, women like this leave those kinds of relationships very bitter concerning men. They believe subconsciously that "payback" is in order. They have to get some kind of revenge on some man that will make them feel better. That is where you as the "good man" come in. These women know that the bad boy could care less if they cheat on him or do anything for that matter. The bad boy is only concerned about himself and getting what he wants. You are the type of guy who actually cares about her and your relationship. That makes you the perfect target!

The Breaking Point is a great book written by **Sue Shellenberger** dealing with the female midlife crisis. She discusses a 3,000 person study done in 2002 by the American National Opinion Centre showing that the overall rate of women who cheat is rising and quickly approaching that of men, with one in six married women saying they have had affairs. Pay attention because this study was done way back in 2002; and there are still plenty of women cheating on their men today. As a matter of fact, I conducted my own nonscientific research and did an independent poll of different women of diverse backgrounds and cultures about this taboo subject. I chose not to go by my own experience or what other men have told me. I wanted the raw unmitigated truth behind why women cheat, and this is what the majority of these women told me.

Why Women Cheat On Their Men

1. Some women cheated on their lovers because they said that the men stopped paying attention to them. *"Don't start what you can't finish"* seemed to be the running theme from them all. They stated that their lovers began the relationship with romance and flowers, but later stopped after she gave up the goods. They all had the opinion that once they have sex with a man, it seems that his interest is no longer as strong and he begins to falter. They love the thrill of being chased and not the feeling of being emotionally dumped after the conquest.

2. The grass appeared to be greener on the other side, and she just had to screw this new guy that aroused her. Surprisingly, some women said that these men reminded them of the men they had at home, but most of them were attracted to these new men because they were different than the men in their lives. The new guys were dangerous and turned them on. Some women want the good guy to be Dad for the kids because he is safe and predictable, but when the romance cools, they want the player to be their "daddy" in bed because he is mysterious.

3. Another reason why women cheat on their men is because the man changed physically, emotionally or both. When some men get comfortable in their relationship, they tend to let themselves go with excessive weight gain from fifteen to even eighty pounds and no longer have that six pack that she fell in love with. Some guys stay physically attractive but begin to mistreat their women and take them for granted. The men become less understanding and the infamous "bitch" word may fly out every now and then. Then there are those fellows who change in both ways, and their women leave them high and dry without delay!

4. A large number of women said that their man cheated first, and revenge was on their mind. This is self explanatory, and I am not going to waste time dealing with it. If you are dumb enough to think that you can cheat on your woman, and get her to just take it and get over it, then you deserve to be by yourself!

5. One of the women I interviewed boldly boasted, *"I am here to spread evil across the world because I feel it is my God-given right to tear a man down and cut off his balls!"* These types of chicks are psychos and should be avoided at all costs! They prey on men and may have some deep- rooted emotional issues dealing with men in their past, or they just get off on destroying good guys.

Whenever I am conducting a seminar, I have had women approach me and say that they pray to God for a "good man" but when they get one they mistreat him to the point where he wishes that he never met her. Some of these women do not know why they do awful things to the good man and others are just malicious like the psychos from my independent study of why women cheat. Here are some examples of this type of unnecessary drama that I heard about at some of my seminars from my students. These examples are from two men who were brave enough to stand up and share with everyone in attendance. I hope that you guys never have to deal with some of these issues, but I am guessing that you probably have. These are examples of women creating drama with their good man.

+ The Actor Debacle: This gentleman and his girlfriend were going to the movies to see a new release from one of her favorite actors. The trailer looked exiting, and he mentioned that he wanted to see the film as well. They went and sat through the film and enjoyed it. He knew that she had a crush on the actor, but he was not intimidated at all about that. Somehow, a comparison between the actor and himself came up. She implied that her boyfriend was more attractive than the actor only by the ears and that their daughter would be more attractive if the actor was the father! I am telling you right now that those words pissed him off to no end! I could not believe that she would say something so cruel and disrespectful to her boyfriend. He explained that he would never do that in a million years because he knows that *the most beautiful woman in the world is the one that you are with,* not some chick on the screen or on the radio! By the way, their daughter is very beautiful and a child model. Go figure!

- The STD: This little example made every man in the place see red while this brother spoke. He described a time before he married his wife. He loved his wife more than anything in this world. Their relationship was going strong, and they were getting closer than they had ever thought. You know, finishing sentences and such. One day he noticed that it hurt when he urinated. He says that it felt like razor blades were coming out whenever he went to the bathroom! He was concerned and went to the clinic. He was informed that he had an STD. The man knew that he was only with her and asked if he could have gotten it from a toilet seat. This poor guy did not want to accept the thought that the love of his life had been with someone else. It hurt him to no end to discover that she had been unfaithful. He further expressed that she had no reason to cheat. It is just what she wanted to do. He was further distraught because he mentioned all the women that he could have cheated on her with, including her sister! He married her anyway and the drama continued.

It is unfortunate that we as men can be very faithful but still get criticized by society to be nothing but low-down dirty dogs. Some of my students feel that there is no hope in being the good guy to women who will do nothing but see them as weak. This can be difficult because I went through the same thing in various relationships. I, too, felt like there was no sense in giving myself to a woman when she would not be faithful and honor our relationship. I went through a lot of unnecessary drama from both my ex-wives way back when they were not the wonderfully wise women they are now. I lovingly call them Uno and Deuce to protect their identities because there are ignorant people out there that would try to crucify them because of their past. These women were gracious and brave enough to allow me to talk about these events, and I still love them. We all go through a cycle of immaturity, and these are some examples of Uno & Deuce creating drama when there was none. All of my immaturity B.S comes later. Trust me; my ex-wives have nothing on me!

I met Uno when I was eighteen in the time that I call "Young & Dumb." This was the time period from my late teens to mid twenties. I found that I made most of my mistakes during this time period when I felt that I was an adult but I still was thinking like a child. I know that I made many mistakes during this time, and I was very immature. Uno and I were young and inexperienced and that novice nature raised its ugly head on more than one occasion! Her dad was a preacher, and I attended their church. I saw how beautiful she was, and I could not help myself. I did not know anything about the legend of the preacher's kid. It states that these children have lived under so many rigid restrictions that they grow up to become wild and crazy. Like I said, I had not heard of that yet, but I would soon find out!

I was an artist, and I liked to draw Japanamation or manga. I had given some of my drawings to Uno to check out. Her father saw them and threw them away because he said that it was not pleasing in the eyes of the Lord! These were my drawings that took me years to do and he tossed them as if they were nothing! They were giant robots like Voltron and Transformers for crying out loud! They were not his to throw away, and I doubt that Jesus whispered in his ear and told him anything! He never apologized for that by the way.

I should have examined the situation closer and seen what I was dealing with. He was a man who held strong to his convictions, and everybody else was wrong except him. His way was the only way to live, and all other opinions were meaningless in his eyes. Only his small church flock was destined for Heaven while all other churches and the rest of humanity were doomed to hell. This is her dad, okay, so imagine how she thinks!

We got married, and I realized that train of thought ran through her as well. She did whatever she wanted, and she would say *"God will just have to forgive me"* if she did anything wrong, as long as she was in church on Sunday. I also want to mention that I was no saint! It doesn't have to be just the preacher's kids; good old-fashioned hypocrites think this way as well-- if the shoe fits!

Things got progressively worse as we procreated. I tried to get along with her family, but I just did not believe in what they did. I did not see her dad as the "know it all" guru behind God that they did. I did not agree with the fact that my in-laws wanted to control my marriage simply because my wife was their daughter. We separated, and the end was near.

It all came to a head when Uno and I had argued over the phone about the kids. I told her that I was coming to see the kids, and she argued that I was not going to see them. They all were at her father's house, and I did not take no for an answer. I pulled up and they all piled out of the house like grunts in the Marine Corps! She stepped out of the house along with her three brothers and her parents along with my kids. Her baby brother brought out his father's shotgun and aimed it at my head! Thank God I didn't die, but I was not willing to back down. My kids were horrified because they thought that their uncle was about to kill their dad. I looked at my kids and eventually used proper judgment and left.

That is something they should have never seen. They are still affected by that incident, even though it is years later. I had to realize that *regardless if I feel that someone is wrong, I need to make the proper decision that will lead to a positive conclusion.* No one has the power to do this in my life but me and me only. Uno created the drama by keeping my kids from me, but I gave the drama strength by going along in a negative way. I get along great with her parents now, and we all have learned valuable lessons of what not to do! If you have problems with visitation because of your ex (it doesn't matter whether you owe child support or are current), then I advise you to go through the courts and cement your rights as a father if you do not have custody.

Let's move on to Deuce, shall we? I met her while I was in the process of divorcing Uno. I was a fledgling music producer at the time, and she came over with a friend of hers to check me out. There was an instant attraction, and let's just say that the night had a happy ending! I did not look at the fact that I had just met this woman, and I was sexing her already. Talk about being "Young & Dumb"! I would never do something like that now if I were trying to see if that particular woman were suitable for marriage. These types of women are the ones you "do and be done with." I hate to say it like that, but a one-night fling is exactly that, a fling for one night!

I enjoyed myself, we talked on the phone constantly, and I wanted to see more of her. We went out a couple of days after our initial meeting, and she stayed the night. It was then that she revealed she was married! I hit the roof! How could she be with me all day and night and have a husband at home with three children? She said it was over between them and that she loved me. Despite her confession, I must admit, I still wanted her. By week two, I was head over hills in love and wanted more from the relationship.

Even when I had an opportunity to get out of the relationship, I stopped her from going. She said we should take it slowly, but I wanted what I wanted, and she was it. Eventually, we became exclusive. I could not see what was clearly in front of me. I should have used better judgment; she was clearly another woman who just had to have her way, regardless of the fact that she was hurting her "good man" at home! This time I was the bad boy on the other end and not the victim. I could have cut her loose; it would have saved us both years of drama, but I did not. Live by the sword as the old adage goes.

I remained involved with her, and we both finalized our divorces. I developed a great relationship with her kids, and they loved my kids. Everything was perfect until the inevitable happened. If you are dating a cheater, one day he or she will cheat on you! She cheated in one way or another throughout our relationship because she felt like she had that right. I could have done the same thing, and I did once or twice, but I stopped the drama on my part because I knew that cheating would not lead to the end of cheating; it leads to more cheating! It takes maturity to "not" do something when you possess the power to "get even." I found it funny that even though she cheated a lot, she was always concerned about my doing it, and some woman taking me away from her and the kids. Ironic, isn't it.

It seems like some women create drama out of nothing. I want to include the up-coming example because this happened recently to another close female friend of mine. I love her like a sister, but she was as dumb as a brick with this one. I'll call her "Brenda" to keep from embarrassing her. Brenda called me and told me that she just had a major fight with her husband "John" and that he had kicked her out of their home.

Apparently, he was upset at her because they were at a corporate picnic sponsored by her job, and there was a certain male co-worker who had his eye on her. She was at the food table getting some ketchup when her co-worker leaned over her with his pelvis on her ass to get the mustard. She laughed as she leaned back on him getting closer to his lower region. All of this was done in front of everyone, including her husband who was sitting at a table ten feet away with their young daughter.

Let's just say her husband got upset and made a scene at the picnic. Brenda later phoned a female friend, "Lisa," who was divorced without a man and told her what happened. Lisa told her that John was out of line, and he should have never made a scene. Now I want you to remember that Lisa did not have a man, and there was a very good reason why. Brenda told Lisa that John had not given her any attention since the picnic, and she wanted some advice.

Lisa proceeded to tell Brenda that she needed to make John jealous to motivate him to spend more time with her. Now here comes the bull squeeze. I want all the women reading this book to pay attention to this simple statement. ***Women should never listen to another woman who does not have a man!*** Misery loves company and just maybe she secretly has her eyes on your man!

Anyway, Lisa told Brenda to go to the male co-worker from the picnic and ask him for a pair of his boxer shorts. Brenda got the shorts and put them in her bed so John could discover them when he came home and think that she was cheating on him! This is so asinine that it makes no sense! If you and your mate are having trust issues, why in the hell would you amplify the situation by making him think that you are cheating on him?! John found the boxer shorts and aggressively kicked her out of the house expeditiously!

Brenda had nowhere to go and called Lisa to tell her what happened. But Lisa was not answering her phone for some mysterious reason, so Brenda called another friend and crashed at her place for a few days. Apparently, some drama went down between Brenda and her friend's husband, so she was subsequently kicked out of there and was back on the street. That's when she decided to call me. When she told me what was going on, I took the liberty of saying that she was a dumb-ass and deserved what she got. There was absolutely no sympathy from me because she had fooled around on John in the past, and she considered him to be weak because he never challenged her bad behavior in their relationship.

I gave some simple advice. I told her to go to her husband in a humble way and beg for his forgiveness. She agreed to do it and said that she would call me after she talked to him. What she didn't tell me is that she had finally gotten in touch with Lisa. Lisa told her to do the exact opposite! She told Brenda to square off against her husband and tell him that he was not handling his business in the bedroom and that she would continue to cheat on him until he got his act together. She went on to say that he should just forgive whatever she decided to do because she was a black woman who had been treated unfairly! Who do you think Brenda decided to listen to? She did what Lisa told her to do!

She got home and her husband welcomed her in with open arms and a freshly prepared meal for her. He was not angry anymore and was in a mood to talk. She ate the meal and decided to give him a piece of her mind. All I know is that dumb-dumb called me saying that she was hiding in the bushes because he got angry and lost his mind! She ran out of the house because he started swinging at her and tossing furniture around in a rage.

Now this situation is the equivalent to hitting a bee hive with a baseball bat! You know the bees are there, and you know what they are going to do to you if you hit the hive. They are going to aggressively attack you because you were stupid enough to mess with them in the first place! I asked Brenda how she could be so stupid as to say that garbage after she was the one disrespecting her marriage and had even cheated on her husband in the past.

She said that she trusted Lisa and that another woman would never steer her wrong! John eventually divorced Brenda, and here's the kicker; he ended up dating Lisa and moving her into the house! Brenda's so-called friend played her like the fool she is, and now Brenda is staying with different men while Lisa is banging John's brains out in Brenda's bed! Retribution is a bitch, but she is fair, and Brenda got what she deserved! And by the way, I hear that John is now cheating on Lisa! Hahahahaha!!!!!!!!!!!!!!

The 4 Way

Another example I like to use in my seminars is what I call the "FOUR WAY". There is a white man married to a white woman, and he is cheating on his wife with a black woman married to a black man. The white man and the black woman both know that the other is married and the white woman knows that her husband has had numerous affairs for years but continues to stay with him and his money, even though she is heart broken. The black man is completely clueless until it is too late.

The slow-to-see-the-obvious brother finds out about the affair and plants his foot in his wife's ass. He is arrested for domestic violence and taken to jail. The question I present to you is who is the most morally wrong. Some people say that clearly the black man is wrong because he committed a "legal" crime and was incarcerated. Some men argue that domestic violence is definitely a legal crime, but his actions broke no moral laws because of the obvious situation of his wife's affair, although plenty of women objected to their argument.

Others said that the white man and the black woman were equally guilty of being the moral perpetrators because they both were married and had the affair anyway. They say that the black man's actions were purely reactionary as a result of his hurt, but the white man and the black woman were on offense the whole time and made the decision to hurt their spouses in the most intimate way. Most of the black women in the group objected to that. They stated that this fiasco was the white man's fault. They shouted out in unison that he was a dog to his wife and obviously seduced the black woman with his money and lured her away from her psycho husband. They said that the black woman was completely blameless and was the victim in the situation.

I'm sure you know that there were individuals in the seminar who were not happy with their answer. The smallest group in the audience was white women. They said that the white woman committed no legal crime and no moral crime because she was not having affairs and betraying her wedding vows like her scumbag of a husband or beating anyone down like that abusive thug. I can tell this touched a nerve because some white women, in a roundabout way, expressed their outrage that the white man was sleeping with a black woman. The sisters in the audience fired back by saying that he was probably cheating because the black woman had more ass than his skinny toothpick white wife. The funny thing is that most of the white guys didn't say anything for fear of the other groups ganging up on them. They just remained silent in all of the commotion.

It is amazing to me that every time I present this situation, I get a wide range of emotion and answers. I had to step in and tell everyone that the scenario was intended to see if I could drive a wedge between them and if they would side with whatever character closely resembled them. I asked everyone to fill out a questionnaire at the beginning of the seminar. I asked the question *"Have you ever been cheated on in a past or current relationship and need closure?"* They all answered yes to the question. Their responses to this situation were likely fueled by the want to see the character that reminded them of themselves to be vindicated because maybe they felt like they themselves needed some sort of vindication.

I expressed that all of the characters were morally wrong. The black man was wrong because he responded inappropriately and found himself locked up. His freedom and good name were stripped from him over a woman who cheated on him. The white man and the black woman were wrong because their moral sins were clear and obvious. The white women looked at me as if I were crazy when I said that the poor little white wife was just as wrong as or more morally wrong than all of them, and this is why.

It is true that the other three characters committed actions against others that were morally wrong. She was morally wrong because she constantly allowed herself to be emotionally abused and refused to do anything about it. She was committing moral sins against herself for her lack of action. Either she loved her husband unconditionally and hoped he would change on his own, or maybe she didn't love herself enough to know that she deserved better. *The greatest crime you can ever commit is to sin against yourself and allow yourself to be destroyed.*

The black man responded to his wife and showed his displeasure with her behavior. He just responded the wrong way, but at least he fought back in a way and refused to be disrespected. He went to jail because he broke the law, and he had to know in the back of his mind while he was beating her that there was a strong chance that he may go away for a while after this. He made the choice to put his hands on her and paid the price.

One thing I want you to always remember, *regardless if I feel that someone is wrong, I need to make the* <u>proper</u> *decision that will lead to a* <u>positive</u> *conclusion.* The black man made the wrong decision and had a negative outcome. The white woman had no response and had an ongoing, negative outcome. She had the power to make it stop, but she refused to act. Nothing positive comes from negativity and absolutely nothing positive comes from inaction! She was just as morally wrong as everybody else because she refused to change her situation! I wanted to talk about that situation to show that I am not biased against women, but this book (especially this chapter) was written for men, after all, as a guide of what not to do when the woman or women in their lives create drama from nothing.

The greatest example I have for women creating drama when there is none is the biblical Eve. She was the queen of an entire planet, had a loving husband and communed directly with her creator. What more could a woman ask for?! She literally had the world at her beck and call but still found a way to create drama where there was none. She listened to a snake that told her that it was okay to eat the forbidden fruit. She knew that God specified that she and Adam could eat everything else with the exception of that one particular tree. This is a classic case of having everything but still wanting more. As a result, according to the Christian tradition, man fell from grace, we now die, and the world is what it is today! She created a whole lot of drama over nothing!

But hold your horses because Adam is equally to blame! God specifically told Adam what NOT to eat because he was supposed to be the leader. The leader is *supposed* to be the responsible member of the group that is *supposed* to know better! Instead of Adam standing up to her and doing the right thing, he chose to partake of the fruit with his wife resulting in the fall of man! **We as men must lead with love and not allow ourselves to succumb to what we know are the wrong judgments or do nothing at all when some sort of action must be taken to stop an**

obviously bad situation! This example also shows how if we continue to allow ourselves to be manipulated by anybody because we love them, we are making a major mistake.

You have the power to stop the drama in your life whether it is coming from a woman, yourself, or other outside influences. So, if you are a good man who was hurt by your ex, stop complaining about it because it does you no good. Instead, actually do something to try and mend the fence if possible and get on with the business of being a great dad! A new, better woman is on the horizon. Just show a little *patience*; remember that word?

7 Kids Challenge # 3: Are you a GOOD Man frustrated with the lousy selection of women in your circle? I challenge you to go out and FLIRT for thirty days! Step out of your comfort zone and confidently approach women you think are out of your league. Don't worry if they shoot you down. The point of the exercise is to build confidence which will improve your self esteem. Through persistence, you will eventually get that one phone number from that goddess of your dreams. Take it slow and see what happens.

4.

AM I KILLING MY KID? : TEEN SUICIDE

"You have the power because you are the dad!"

Being a single dad in today's world can be challenging. You have to deal with all the bills and have sole responsibility for that bundle of joy that you brought into the world. Your children start off so precious and cute as babies, and then they grow up! They get boyfriends or girlfriends, hang out with the wrong people, experiment with illegal drugs and alcohol, or get pregnant! These are those very tough issues that all parents have to face at some time.

Single fathers are no different than anybody else. They have to directly deal with these issues like any other parent, and I am saddened to say that the single father demographic is growing exponentially around the world and moving at a greater pace here in the U.S. I would love to see all families stay together. But if you are a single father, then I encourage you to be the very best parent because your kids deserve it.

The U.S. Census Bureau reported that there are over 2.5 million single fathers residing in the United States and that number is up from just under 400,000 in 1970. 19% of all single parents in America are men who have dedicated themselves to their children and are focused on maintaining strong, wholesome environments for their family. Among these fathers, 8% are raising three or more children younger than 18 years old, 40% are divorced or never married, 16% are separated, 4% are widowed, 14% live in someone else's home and 27% have an annual income of $50,000 or more.

The silver lining in the dark cloud of broken homes is that dads are finally starting to receive child support as well. In a recent study, custodial fathers received 2.1 billion in child support but were owed 3.3 billion. Unfortunately, the government does not crack the whip as hard when absentee mothers are delinquent on their payments. The census also showed that single mothers received 23 billion in child support, and we all know what happens to men who are late on their payments! The courts will hall you off to jail (no questions asked), suspend your driver's license, and hit you with a hefty fine.

In most cases, the man stays in jail because he cannot afford to bail himself out. He then loses his job because he did not report to work and companies quickly fire people who have been arrested for anything! He cannot get another job because his arrest pops up on his background when other employers run a background check. Newsflash! "YOU DO NOT HAVE TO BE CONVICTED OF ANYTHING...JUST AN ARREST ON YOUR RECORD IS ENOUGH TO DISQUALIFY YOU FROM MOST COMPANIES!" This is an absolute fact! If you are black, white, Jew, Gentile and everything in between; any man behind on his child support will suffer the consequences! I urge all of you to stay current or ahead on your child support because your ass is grass if you don't!

The Canace Curse

Single fathers have been targeted and some critics speculate that men are not equipped with the necessary emotional prowess to deal with parental issues. I personally feel that these so-called experts are wrong, but we as fathers have a lot to prove. Unfortunately, some of us prove these people right.

Deuce told me a story a while back about a young woman named Canace (Can-ah-see). She is a part of Greek mythology and she had an overbearing dad named Aeolus (Ye-oh-lus). Aeolus was quite a significant character in the ancient world. He is best known for being the king in the Homer's Greek epic poem *The Odyssey* who gave Odysseus a tightly closed bag full of captured winds for his long journey home. He was a powerful king who was in good favor with the gods, and when he spoke, people listened. His power and influence were very intimidating to most, especially to Canace. This story is a great example for teaching fathers to look at different ways to handle their children and themselves in a time of crisis.

Aeolus was a great and legendary king, but he sucked as a dad, and this is why. His little darling daughter Canace fell in love with a handsome fellow and got pregnant. The problem is that the fellow was her brother Macareus! As you can imagine, Aeolus was livid when he found out. He was so mad, he ordered the child to be killed only minutes after its birth, literally throwing it out to the wolves. He then sent one of his servants to Canace with a sword ordering her to commit suicide as a punishment for such immoral behavior.

Now I know that you would never tell your kids to commit suicide if they did something that disappointed you; however, some kids feel like killing themselves because they know how you would react if they did something wrong. Many of these kids are killing themselves because of us, the parents!

I had difficulty sleeping one night as I was so troubled by the ugliness of teen suicide and the real impact that it has on our kids. After downing two espressos, I searched the web and came across the **National Alliance on Mental Illness (NAMI)** website. It provides so much great information on spotting the signs and how to treat teen suicide. What startled me is when I read that in 1996 more teens and young adults died from suicide than pneumonia, birth defects, stroke, heart disease, influenza, chronic lung disease, cancer and AIDS combined!

Gay teens tend to fly below the radar of most statistics, but they are responsible for 35% of all attempts and actual suicides of kids between fourteen and twenty-one. *Jim Foster* is an expert on the subject and he says *"It's because of internalized homophobia, sexual-identity issues, and isolation. These kids don't dare open up to anyone. They may think it's acceptable in society to come out, but it's not safe. Then they get into despair, and gay teen depression is lethal."*

Another endangered demographic is in the African American community. **According to NAMI, from 1980 to 1996, the rate of suicide among African-American males aged 15 to 19 years increased by 105 percent!** I was not surprised to learn that the number of young black men who attempt or complete suicide is rising quickly due to high rates of divorce, fatherless homes and living in low-income environments. These teens have a grim philosophy on life and feel that the world hates them or is rooting against them because they are black.

The negative images that are portrayed about black men have had an effect on how society views and treats them. Being a black man who grew up in the late 20th century, I had to struggle internally with what direction I was going in. Would I succumb to the negative stereotype and kill myself or overcome my adversity and make something of myself? This is a problem that is destroying ALL races of children in the next generation on a global scale!

When I was in college, I had a good friend from Korea, and I was the first black person whom he had met. He was shocked because I was articulate and didn't try to rob him. He admitted to being worried when he first met me because all he was fed as a kid living in Korea during the early eighties was that black men were evil rapist, thieves and murderers! He was conditioned by watching American news casts depicting black men being arrested for all the crimes. *"I never saw white people being hauled away to jail, just blacks. White people never commit crimes in America."* he told me one day. This ignorance is what was being taught in his village! One should not have to wonder why young black males are tempted more often to take their lives when they have to convince the whole world that they are not the spawns of Satan!

Here is where teen suicide and the Canace Curse ties in. Deuce told me another story about a friend's cousin who killed herself. She was in high school, a preacher's kid, and had gotten pregnant. She was afraid to tell her dad. Imagine the fear and pain that ran through this young lady's mind as she contemplated revealing her secret. She knew that this was something that she could not keep to herself for long because she would start showing after awhile. She went to her boyfriend and told him that she was pregnant. What do you think the boyfriend said to her? I will let you ponder it for a second. You guessed it; he was not ready to settle down, and he was too young to be a father.

They planned a way for her to get an abortion, but the plans fell through. She felt she had no one to turn to, and in her mind she was trapped. There was no way she was telling her father. Unfortunately, this little girl's solution to her problem was to walk outside to her dads' truck with his shotgun, sit down inside, and shoot herself in the head. She killed herself because she felt her dad could not cope and deal with the situation. She needed her dad to be there for her and not damn her to Hell because of a mistake.

Who knows, he may have handled the situation differently after the initial anger passed, but she was so afraid due to past encounters with him they will never know. His rigidness over the years, in an effort to raise her the Christian way, (I am not saying there is anything wrong with teaching children God's way) put them in a place where the lines of communication were closed, being replaced by rules and regulations. This goes parallel with the Canace story. Aeolus would not listen or try to understand and fix the problem; he just reacted out of emotion, resulting in the death of Canace and his grandchild.

In the example above, the father would have responded similarly to Aeolus as far as his daughter was concerned. In her mind, he would have been extremely disappointed with her and would have let it be known. He did not put the gun in her hand physically, like Aeolus with the sword, but he put it there psychologically. She felt that since she was such a disappointment to her dad that she would rather end her life than to face him.

How important are you dad? Is this happening to your child?

This problem is compounded by the number of "Copy Cat" deaths that follow a successful suicide called the Cluster Effect. **Dr. Pamela Cantor** frequently lectures at Harvard Medical School, and is an expert in adolescent suicide, and she says, *"Kids see that this is a glamorous way to die, a way to get a lot of attention that they couldn't get in life."* She continues, *"They see a kid that is a nonentity suddenly get attention, and that is what they have been struggling for."* We have to understand the power that we have as parents, and be careful how we direct that power.

We as parents must also recognize possible signs in our children that they may be contemplating suicide. This may be difficult at times because WE are in denial that this could not be happening with OUR child. Let's take the blinders off and look at some common symptoms that your child may be showing.

- Extreme personality changes
- Loss of interest in activities that used to be enjoyable
- Significant loss or gain in appetite
- Difficulty falling asleep or wanting to sleep all day
- Fatigue or loss of energy
- Feelings of worthlessness or guilt
- Withdrawal from family and friends
- Neglect of personal appearance or hygiene
- Sadness, irritability, or indifference
- Having trouble concentrating
- Extreme anxiety or panic

+ Drug or alcohol use or abuse
+ Aggressive, destructive, or defiant behavior
+ Poor school performance
+ Hallucinations or unusual beliefs
+ Putting one's affairs in order, such as giving or throwing away favorite belongings
+ Talks about dieing to friends or writes about it in a diary or e-mail

If your child is exhibiting these behaviors you may need to take immediate action. The first step is to talk to them. Let them know how important they are to you. Sometimes just acknowledging a kid and telling them how much they are loved, respected and needed can make them feel better for the moment. I encourage you to call the **NAMI Help Line at 1-800-950-NAMI (6264)** for more detailed information.

Quite a few years ago when I was no longer with Uno and Deuce had just gone through labor and birthed little number seven; I understood that having another child would be a delicate situation for my older children with Uno. I had to be there for my new baby, but I also had an obligation to secure my older children's position in my heart without making them feel shut out and abandoned. After having my own teen suicidal issues when I was a kid, I knew first hand that children will feel abandoned when their father remarries and starts a new family. I did not want my children to become statistics so I had to figure out how to make this an easier transition for them.

There was a rift between Uno and myself at the time, and she started making life difficult for me. The fact that I had moved on did not concern her, but my actually having a child with someone else struck a nerve. She always prided herself in being able to say, *"I'm the mother of your children, and those other chicks are not important."* That phrase of hers was no longer true, and reality set in and hit her like a ton of bricks. That is when I realized that she was just as hurt about our divorce as I was. She had covered up her feelings all this time, and now she could not hide behind her mask anymore. I can't say that I blame her.

Being the product of a divorced home, I understood the importance of making my kids feel equally important and loved. My father left my mom and moved on with several women. He had other children, and I felt abandoned and unloved. This was hard for me because I was just a kid and needed him. I felt like I was thrown away and unwanted by my father and did not deserve to be loved by anyone. Only within the last five years have I been able to let that old pain go and forgive my dad for leaving me. But some children do not have the strength to do this as they blame themselves for their new broken family.

It is your job to be proactive in helping your children heal from a broken home and mend fences with your former spouse. Let her know from the beginning that the protection, happiness and stability of your kids are more important than some old, sour feelings between the two of you. You must come to an agreement to work together before it is too late.

7Kids Challenge # 4: Do you think your child may be suicidal? I challenge you to get together with your former spouse and have a family meeting with your kids. Discuss how important they are to you both and that they are loved. Tell them that they are not the cause of the divorce, but they are the reason why their combative parents can finally stop bickering and learn how to get along.

5.

THE DARK SIDE OF LOVE: CHILD ABUSE, CHILD RAPE AND DOMESTIC VIOLENCE

"Sometimes we need to look in the mirror to see where our problems lie and know that there are no perfect people, including ourselves."

I WANT TO SHARE with you a very sad story about a little boy that was constantly abused by his mother. She would slap him around the house simply for looking too much like his father. There was an incident when she chocked him under the Christmas tree until he passed out because he wanted to see his father. He would wake up to her standing over him with a knife to his throat; she attempted to drown the boy in the bath tub because he got a "B" on his report card, and she had broken his leg and arm in a fit of rage. This poor child now suffers from Depression, low self-esteem, Post Traumatic Stress Disorder (PTSD), violent nature and Multiple Personality Disorder. This is what can happen to a child that grows up in an abusive household. What angers me is that his father knew that he was being abused but didn't give a damn! He did nothing as his ex-wife tortured his child! It's time for men to stand up and protect their kids from ALL harm!

How important are you dad? Is this happening to your child?

Sometimes as good parents we have to pay close attention to our children because they may not be willing to tell us that something is wrong. Most children do not tell when they are being abused. The abuser manipulates the child into thinking that he or she did something wrong and deserves to be punished. The abuser uses fear and threats to control the child and keep him or her silent. The child does not want the abuse to continue or for anyone else to get hurt. This can be very hard to spot. I had to learn from my own experience that children may be too afraid to tell the truth.

In 1985, I was raped by a man whom I call "The Wicked Man" when my mom sent me to camp. He was a male counselor, and he forced me into a cabin and made me perform oral sex on him! Most people consider this gruesome act molestation, but I use the word rape because he had his hand around my neck choking me and violently forced me to do something that I didn't want to do! He made me feel powerless! This bastard took advantage of an eleven-year-old little boy who could not fight back! The sickest part of it all is that he told me that he was raped by a priest when he was a child, and he was led by God to do it to me!

I remember him whispering in my ear, *"He did it to me, and he was a man of God. Surely it was ok to God for him to have me, so you know the Lord wants me to have you. This is God's will; don't fight it."* He also told me that if I screamed he would kill me, and if I ever told anyone that he would hunt me down and kill both me and my mom by cutting off our heads! Tears flowed down my cheeks heavily as he forced his penis in my mouth. He then pushed me off him complaining that I was not doing it right! I took that brief moment and bolted out of the cabin. He did this to me on the last day of camp, and I was ready to get on that bus and go home! The other kids on the bus all wondered what was wrong with me, but I didn't say a word. After I got home, I was too afraid to tell my mom because of his threat, and I thought that it was somehow my fault.

I don't know who to blame anymore. Do I blame the guy who raped me, or blame the priest who raped him and filled his head with idiotic religious dogma to justify his act?! All I know is that I felt hopeless, ashamed and seriously questioned if God loved me. As a grown man, I know that God had nothing to do with the evil desires of two perverts who preyed on children. But as I grew up and held on to this painful secret, I often found myself wondering why a loving God would allow this to happen to me.

I remember attempting to call my father to tell him what happened at camp. I figured that God had forgotten me and surely my dad would have my back. He had not been in my life for several years at this point but I needed to hear some comforting words from him. I just knew in my mind that my mother must be forcing him to stay away from me because every time I wanted to see him, he was always too busy. Mom did not know that I had looked in her purse and copied down his phone number. I secretly called him from the bathroom for a week until he finally picked up.

I cried on the phone as I relived the rape and begged for him to pick me up. He hesitated for a few moments and finally said that he was on his way. I dried my tears and waited anxiously for my dad. I thought to myself, *"I knew mom was lying when she said dad didn't care about me! He's on his way right now to make me feel better!"* It seemed time intentionally moved slowly as I waited. Three hours had passed by and still no sign of my father. I called his phone, but there was no answer. I patiently waited another four hours before I eventually gave up. My father never showed up that day. I did not hear from my father for three years! At that point, it was too late. I realized God never forgot me, but my dad definitely did.

I developed a strong hatred for my father after that incident. My mother always told me that he did not care about me, and she was right. I decided to never tell the truth about what happened to me. I realized that my father would not protect me or my mother from the Wicked Man if I did tell. I could not count on my dad to do his job and support me when I needed him the most! I was afraid to tell the truth, and I never told my mother that I was raped until I was thirty-three years old.

How important are you dad? Is this happening to your child?

It can be difficult to spot child abuse because clothing may cover up the marks and the child often will not tell. It is up to adults to bring this to light and get that child out of danger. Here are some questions that can help you identify an abused child:

+ Does the child display anger, becomes withdrawn from others, jumpy or anxious, distrustful, or seems to carry an immense burden of guilt?

+ Did the child's behavior in school and school work suddenly change?

+ Does the child suddenly feel like he or she has to be perfect and overly respectful?

+ Does the child display inappropriate, sexually explicit, adult-like behavior?

+ Is the child reluctant to go home?

These signs can be hard to see at times and in no way am I suggesting that every child displaying every sign is being abused. But over **3,195,000** cases of child abuse and neglect have been reported, and fifteen out of every 1,000 children are being abused while over **1,200** children are killed each year. It is in every child's best interest for you to look into the matter. If you find evidence of abuse, please call the police. You can remain anonymous if you tell a teacher, child protective services, or even your doctor. These professionals know how to get the child some help. Some children confide in someone they trust. Be sure to tell them that they are brave and they are doing the right thing. It is not nor has it ever been their fault. Finally, you can call the **NATIONAL CHILD ABUSE HOTLINE AT 800-422-4453.**

I said all of this because certain behaviors are passed down from parents to their kids. I told you earlier that your children would emulate you. The remaining part of this chapter is going to focus on how responding inappropriately to what I call emotional attacks from your lover will hurt you more than it hurts them, even if you feel that they deserve it! Your kids record and imitate everything that they see you do. You are teaching them how to solve problems by your actions; NOT your words. Keep that in mind next time you lose your temper.

A friend of mine was having trouble in his marriage. His wife cheated on him with a married man and gave him a very serious sexually transmitted disease. It angered him to no end. He had told her in the beginning of their relationship that his former girlfriend had broken his heart. She looked him in his eyes and promised to never cheat on him. She had now taken advantage of his trust and committed the same horrible crime as the woman before. He felt like a patsy and wanted to get even. She was dead wrong for what she did, but it is irrelevant because the important lesson to learn here is the mistake he made in response. He grew up in an abusive home watching his father beat his mother. He never thought that he would doom himself to the same mistake.

He went to her job to pick her up and did not say anything as she got in the car. His wife knew that something was wrong, but she remained quiet. They got to their home and went to the kitchen. He asked her if there was anything that she needed to tell him. She said no with a worried look on her face. She started walking towards the backdoor, but he stepped in front of her to cut her off. His wife started to cry and that confirmed it! He lost his mind in a fit of rage and tossed her around like a rag doll! He was tired of being hurt and decided to fight back. Unfortunately, he was acting just like his dad! He looked down at the woman with whom he was in love; she was beaten, bruised and crying on the kitchen floor, and he knew that he did it! All he remembered were those countless times of seeing his father beating his mother and how he hated it. He could not deal with the fact that he had now become what he despised the most…a monster.

Over the years, they tried to work it out, but they both continued their trend of hurting each other, tit for tat. For a while, it seemed as though she liked getting her ass kicked knowing if she stepped out on him what the consequences would be. I could not understand a woman intentionally screwing up, knowing she would have to face his wrath. He decided to toss her around a few times one particular day because his pride was hurt stemming from her past sins, and he needed to feel better.

To his surprise, he turned around and saw his children looking at him in total fear. He was dragging their mom around the living room by her hair for absolutely nothing! They heard their mom kicking and screaming and wanted to check on her. I will forever regret not intervening after seeing the pattern that was forming because the situation spiraled out of control. His children had now seen firsthand the monster that was in their father. Absolute terror was on their faces as they saw their mother on the floor crying in pain.

Men, I want you to remember that if it gets this bad with you and your woman, nobody cares what she did to you when they can clearly see what you just did to her! They don't see you crying inside from the pain when the bruises on her are staring them in the face! He made the mistake of beating his wife (just like his dad) because she hurt him. He was arrested, and his wife is still a whore. The ultimate sadness is that many years later, his son (now nineteen years old) is following in his footsteps and has become a domestic offender as well! Like father...like son...like father...like son. When is it going to stop?

I want to make it absolutely clear that I am not giving women a free pass to cheat on their lovers. I completely detest a man putting his hands on a woman, and I also believe that women who wreck men for no reason will ultimately get what's coming to them. I have seen and lived the ugliness that it brings as it rips families apart. It would be irresponsible of me not to mention that some women have a problem with domestic violence as well. These ladies believe that they can slap their man around because he promised to never hit them back. It is disrespectful, and they are taking advantage of their men. This is both dangerous and can be very deadly if he decides that enough is enough and snaps!

Another friend of mine was married to the aforementioned type of abusive woman. His wife was raised in a fatherless home and was molested by her uncle when she was a child and had had a very bad taste in her mouth about men ever since. She hated her father and felt that he should have been there to protect her.

How important are you dad? Is this happening to your child?

She loved her husband, but every time they made love, all she felt was her uncle on top of her as painful memories of the molestation flooded her mind. They were in counseling for a while, but it was unsuccessful as year after year rolled by. The more time passed, the angrier she got, and her rage spewed out against her husband. She refused to acknowledge that she was married to a loving man who dedicated his life to her and their kids. ALL men were evil in her mind, including her husband who was guilty of nothing!

The marriage grew bitter after she started slapping him when he would come home from work. The accusations of him having an affair were rampant and relentless. She would slap him, punch him repeatedly and then kick him to the point at which he had to physically restrain her from hitting him. Her rage grew to the point that she grabbed a kitchen knife and sliced him across his back while he was sleeping. He awakened in agony seeing that his wife wanted to finish him off. He ran out of the house nude and called the police.

She was arrested and yelled out that he was a punk because he never hit her back! She said that he was weak because he showed restraint! He clearly handled the situation correctly, but she failed miserably. Men do not have an excuse to beat their wives, and the same rules apply to women who try to murder their husbands! You have a right to protect yourself. If it gets to be this bad, leave the relationship immediately!

I completely understand the feeling of staying in a troubled relationship when it is clear that it is dangerous and not good for you. Both of my ex-wives cheated on me. They both hurt me and broke my heart into a million pieces. I had my faults as well, and I recognize my role in both failed marriages. I WAS NO SAINT IN EITHER MARRIAGE! My temper was notoriously bad and I adopted the "I don't give a damn" attitude. I responded to both of their infidelities by sleeping with as many friends of theirs as I could. I flaunted my conquests in their faces for crying out loud. That in itself is abuse!

This was not productive as it created a deeper wedge between them and me. You would think that once I did this garbage to Uno and it did not help the marriage, I would not respond the same way to Deuce thinking that somehow things would be different in my second marriage. I was out of control, and things could have gotten a lot worse if I had not finally wised up! I had to understand that no matter how much I was hurting that two wrongs truly do not make a right. *I suffered, my ex-wives suffered and, above all, my children suffered because I did not know how to respond appropriately!* It was never taught to me. Instead of going through all of that drama, I should have just left them alone and found someone who wanted me. It could not have been that hard. I live in Atlanta, and the male to female ratio here is thirty ladies for every one guy. Do the math!

Domestic violence is NEVER the answer to anything! Unfortunately, it may be hard to tell if we are dating a potential batterer. I have provided a set of questions below that I want you to answer honestly. If your spouse or someone you are dating displays any combination of these signs, he or she may be a potential batterer:

+ Is he or she pressuring you for an exclusive commitment immediately?
+ Is he or she excessively possessive?
+ Does he or she have a controlling behavior?
+ Does he or she have unrealistic expectations of you?
+ Has he or she cut you off from family and friends?
+ Does he or she always blame others and you for their mistakes?
+ Is he or she easily insulted?
+ Was he or she abused as a child or raised in a violent family?
+ Is he or she cruel to children or animals?
+ Is he or she verbally abusive?
+ Does he or she enjoy dominating others and forcing them to submit?
+ Has he or she abused others in the past?
+ Does he or she have sudden mood swings?
+ Does he or she threaten violence against you?

People who have these signs are not evil. They may potentially do bad things and are in need of help. To protect yourself, I suggest that you take any new relationship slowly. Tell your friends, parents and loved ones whom you are dating. It would be a good idea for them to meet this person, so they can know who he or she is. Secret relationships hardly ever end well. Listen to any concerns from loved ones you can trust who only have the best intentions for you. Outsiders can sometimes see what you cannot. Go on group dates in public places where plenty of people are around. Never get in any car of a stranger!

And when it comes to sex, "NO MEANS NO!!!" This is not a game. Do not give out mixed signals. And remember that no one has a right to force you to have sex at any time. I want to break this particular situation down further. Some women (not all) like to play games. They like the high of manipulating a man and teasing him. They wait until all the clothes are off, and everything gets hot and heavy. They beckon for men to make passionate love to them, allow penetration and then push them off laughing, claiming they are not ready.

I repeat, THIS IS NOT A GAME, AND IT IS NOT FUNNY! There are cases in which women are legitimately raped this way, and they don't find it funny either. Do not play with someone's emotions. It can lead to a violent rape and abuse. Women have a right to refuse sex at any time, before during or after. But I implore you; if you are one of those women who thinks this situation is funny, please stop. I do not want you to become another statistic!

I want to talk to all domestic offenders, men and women alike. You may be dealing with similar issues in your life at this point, and now you realize that you have to stop and make a radical change for the sake of you and your family. You are smart enough to realize that this type of destructive behavior cannot go on. The first step to your recovery is a critical self analysis. Look at yourself for who you are and focus on the type of person that you want to be. Examine all the ugliness and filth in your life. Look at everything that you are deeply ashamed of, and discover why this behavior is dominant in your life.

It is a fact that most domestic offenders were abused earlier in their life. This type of behavior is processed, learned and then imitated by its victims. I want you to realize that most people will not understand you or care that you were abused and manipulated. All they see is what you are doing to others. It is not fair, but it is the way that it is. You have to take control and fix this before it consumes your life and destroys you from within. Every tear that you shed, every ounce of pain that you endured from your past will tempt you to assault anyone that you think is a threat to you. The relived experience of feeling weak and helpless as some asshole took advantage of you is a feeling that you never want to resurface. But you have to understand by losing control, you are damning yourself to that same pit in hell reserved for that coward who violated you! It is going to be tough, but the time for change is now!

In this chapter, I have discussed some very awful events in my life and in the lives of others. Some of my associates warned me not to include this material in the book, but I want you to be aware of how patterns work within us and our children. I know that there are many ignorant people out there, who may attack me, especially for the awful incident of sexual abuse I suffered as a child, but I was a child, and I really do not care about other people's opinions. I had to fix these serious issues within me in order to gain the love and respect of Uno, Deuce and my kids. Now I have no drama with them! That is the most important thing to me, not what other people think of me!

I want you to think about the things that have gone on in your life that are affecting you negatively today. Our past confirms our present, and our present determines our future.

PAST + PRESENT = FUTURE

1. What past events have hurt you in your life?

2. What negative things have you done in response?

3. How are you going to face your past and change your present to determine a better future?

I want you to put this book down for a moment and ponder these questions. Afterward, I want you to conclude that you have the power to change everything around you. This stuff works! If I can positively deal with my past, rearrange my present to determine a great, prosperous future, you can to! It is not too late for you. I am not going to preach to you, but I have presented facts and told you about my struggle. I had to take off the blinders of denial and open my eyes to kill the negativity within. I have stated what it took for me to change my ways so that I do not become like the people who hurt me. It is up to you to do the same.

7 Kids Challenge # 5: Are you a domestic offender? It is a fact that people who are abused may potentially become abusers. If you are being abused, I challenge you to leave the situation immediately and get to safety! If you are an abuser, I strongly challenge you to STOP! 9 times out of 10, you were abused earlier in life and you are now lashing out that pain. Please know that this behavior is wrong and it will destroy you. I urge you to get the help that you need for the well being of you and your family. You can overcome this. I have faith in you!

6.

GOOD PARENTING, REGARDLESS OF THE LAW!

"You should never allow your children to hold you hostage in your own home!"

RUMOR HAS IT THAT California may pass a law stating that it is illegal to spank your child! A parent will be arrested for 1 year and fined up to a thousand dollars for every offense! What in the world are the people smoking out west! Being a survivor of child abuse, I agree that we need provisions to protect kids from abusive parents and predators, but this is going too far. When the government sticks its nose into our business and starts arresting parents for disciplining their children, nothing good can ever come from it. It is not the government's business to strip away a parent's parental authority!

I live in Georgia, and in the particular county where I live there is a high rate of gang activity. These gangs just popped up and came from nowhere. I have never seen so many suburban faux gangsters in my life!

These kids come from affluent neighborhoods; have well-to- do parents, and drive cars with those monster rims, blinding me in the sun light! They are nowhere near poor or lacking in anything! It is sad when even the rich, white kids want to be ghetto! None of these spoiled brats have any sense of direction, and their parents are afraid of them! Somewhere along the line, their parents gave up their authority and let these children run amuck. I think it is sad that whenever some teenager commits a crime, the police always ask, *"Where are the parents?"* Well, I will tell you where the good parents are; they are locked up in jail!

I mentioned earlier that the lack of fathering causes chaos. Most of these kids come from fatherless homes, and their moms are either afraid of them or just want them to leave, so they can have some peace and quiet. They have no father figure because Dad left a long time ago, leaving a mess that we have to clean up! Do you remember those awful statistics that I mentioned earlier about the fatherless homes? Let me rehash them for you. Children from fatherless homes: 63% of children committing suicide, 90% of all homeless and runaway children, 70% of youths incarcerated, 71% of all high school dropouts, 80% of rapists, 85% of all children who show behavior disorders, and 85% of all youths in prison! Do us all a favor Dad; stick around and raise your kids! There is nothing more disheartening for us as a society than to clean up what you spilled! I repeat; you have the power because you are the dad!

After our divorce, Deuce and I reconciled and broke up again repeatedly until we both got so sick of the merry-go-round that we agreed to leave each other alone for good. During one of our "together cycles," I remember when my youngest step-son, who was fourteen-year-old at the time (#3 of the 7 kids), thought that he was too big for his britches, and

I had to handle him. I will start by saying that he was and still is a great kid, but he decided to test me one particular fall morning.

He was having trouble in school, and he began lashing out at his teacher. Let's just say that he used a whole lot of colorful metaphors! He was sent home and gave the school bus driver a piece of his mind as well. The old "f*^k you" seemed to resurface repeatedly out of his mouth to whomever was unfortunate enough to cross his path. Deuce spoke to him when he got home, and I stayed out of it.

Now back to that lovely fall morning. #3 was always late for school so I decided to make sure that he got up and out of the house on time. I opened the door to his room and noticed that he was sitting on his bed watching television instead of getting ready for school. Now this was what he always did in the morning, and every morning he was late. I told him to cut off the television and get ready for school. I walked away to check on one of the other children and when I returned to check his progress, the television was still on!

I questioned him as to why the television was still on after I said to turn it off. Instead of going the common sense route and just doing as instructed and continuing to prepare for school, he decided to ask me "why" as he stood there brushing his hair. I was taken aback because even though he was currently disrespecting the females in his life, he had not been so bold as to bring it to me. The next thing I hear is Deuce yelling at him about disrespecting me and to do it because I said so, adding that he needed to remember his role in the parent- child relationship. She then left the room, and this is when he lost his mind.

I asked him if at the age of fourteen he felt he was an adult, if he felt he was a man now. Apparently, if he felt he could stand in my face and decide to tell me what he was and was not going to do, he must have felt like he was a man, so it was time for me to handle him accordingly. At six feet tall, 180 pounds, this young man was not about to stand there and take a spanking like in the days of old. He had a very smug attitude and meant every word he said. I asked him once more if he was a man now. His response was to talk back to me while rolling his eyes!

I looked at my son, took a deep breath, and told him to stand down and do what he was told. He got in my face, stared me in the eyes and said "F^#K YOU!" My child was out of line and disrespectful! No child should ever say that BULLSH*T to his or her parents! Therefore, I put my hands on him in a loving but stern way as he hit the floor! I did not hit him, but I snatched him up and slammed him to the floor so fast that he did not know which way was up! I put my knee in his back and my forearm behind his head to pin him down. That is when I reminded him that I was the parent, and he was the child! I am not a "Cup Cake Daddy" who would allow this manner of disrespect in my house!

The house was in frenzy because I had just laid down the law on one of the children. I let him up slowly, and he had a little blood coming from his mouth that dried up within a few seconds. *"F*^k you!"* he shouted again as he ran out of the house. *"You better run, you little bastard!"* I responded out of frustration. That was so wrong; I know this okay. I do not know where he went, and all he had on was a pair of pants, no shirt or shoes. Regardless of how disrespectful my son was at the time, I was worried about him. Consequently, I called the police to help me find my lost child. That was a huge mistake! ***Never involve the cops in domestic issues if you can help it!*** I want to say to all of my white readers that calling the police, even if you are in the right, always seems to turn out badly for minorities, especially black folks! Can I get an Amen from the choir!!!!

Anyway, the boys in blue showed up, I told them what happened, and my kid was found shortly after that. The police officers told my son that he was wrong to disrespect his parents and how they remembered their fathers taking them to the woodshed back in the day when they decided that they were too big for their britches. I told them that I would not allow any of my children to disrespect me or especially their mother. I further explained that #3 had cursed out his teacher and bus driver and that I had to end these VERBALLY VIOLENT outbursts before he hurt himself or someone else.

The officers agreed with what I did! One even said, *"I would have gone much further than that if it was my son. He's lucky you're not like Marvin Gaye's daddy!"* If you do not know, Marvin Gaye was shot and killed by his father for disrespecting him in his house. They then examined #3 and saw that his lip was swollen and saw the small bit of dried up blood he spit on the carpet upon getting up. That is when the handcuffs came out, and they arrested me for simple-battery!

I should have expected this. But in my mind, I could not believe what was happening. This is just simply how the law works. The officers said that they had no choice but to arrest me because of the blood and the fact that the minor had a physical injury, referring to the swollen lip. I sat in the back of the squad car and listened as reports of teenagers breaking into homes and gang shootings were being reported. The officer driving was complaining about how all this gang activity was making his job harder. He said that it was a real shame that these kids were running around like that causing terror in the community.

He kept yelling, "*Where are the parents? These kids are out of control! Why are these so-called parents allowing their children to do this? When are they going to stand up and put their kids in their place?*" I laughed aloud and said that all the good parents were in jail because the police kept putting us there! He just shook his head and said that sometimes he hated his job!

While I was in the joint, I had to defend myself from some guys who were affiliated with a gang. My food was thrown on the floor as they tried to test me. Let's just say that I defended myself and they left me the hell alone after that! Five long days later, when I had finally got out, I had lost my job, my Lexus had been repossessed, and I had a criminal record. To top it all off, I found out that while I was locked up, my step-son was having a great time at his dad's house playing video games and Deuce had had a deep conversation with her ex about how she would not mind being his wife again one day if she outlived me and if he outlived his wife! This was her little way of trying to make up for all the lying and cheating she did to him in their relationship!

This is where Deuce kept on screwing up! She was so busy thinking about her ex-husband that she was clearly not thinking about me! Hello, I am supposed to be your man right now at this time before we broke up again! Why was she in his face? She always destroyed her present because she always concentrated on the past! Apologizing and moving on was one thing, but what the hell was this?! Apparently, my step-son was not the only one to lose his mind and be disrespectful! I'm sure that she would not appreciate it if I were in Uno's face telling her how I still loved her and wanted to get back with her when Deuce died!

Give me a break! She seemed to forget that I was the primary father figure for her kids for years! Their dad was there when he could be, but I was there every day! All that ran through my mind was, *"I can't believe this bullsh*t!"* I wondered if she was planning to kill me, so she could go back to her ex-husband sooner! I can understand dealing with drama from one of your own natural children, but when it comes from a step-child and your so-called woman is out doing just straight crap (I'm trying my hardest not to use too many cuss words in this book), it can be all out hell! I felt disrespected, unappreciated, and I was extremely hurt. Here I am getting thrown in jail for trying to keep order in the house, and my woman is in another man's face! I know a lot of men can identify with me on this one! But I have forgiven Deuce, and we're all good now, so let's move on.

Deuce tried to fix the situation by taking #3 to the same jail where I spent the worst five days of my life. It turned out that they were conducting a "Scared Straight Program." He got to experience for a few hours the hell I went through, all the way down to the inmate jumpsuit to the crappy food. It actually worked! That young man walked out of there understanding what he had done, and he apologized to me face to face. He told me how much he loved me for being a second dad to him and dealing with his drama for so many years. He stated that it had to be hard to be a dad but especially hard to be a step-dad. He respected me for stepping up to the plate to love, cherish and even get locked-up over children that were not mine. He cried as I embraced him and told him that he was always mine since the day I met him when he was just a little boy. I had my son back!

Things started to clear up and a ray of hope slowly seeped through the dark clouds of this mess. The county informed me that the judge tossed my case to the side and did not want me to do any further jail time because he thought that it was ridiculous and wasted his time. He enrolled me in a program where I had to complete some self-awareness classes. Upon completion, my record would be expunged. I completed the classes but had to wait two years before my record was cleared! It took that long for the county to process the paper work! I could not get a good job to save my life because my arrest popped up every time a company did a background check! Therefore, I had to suck it up, toss aside my pride, and deliver pizzas until it was taken off. I hated this, but at least I had some income coming in.

This situation was extremely difficult for me, but I made it through. Deuce paid my fine, I got the certificate, and my record was eventually cleared. She came through for me after breaking my heart yet again. The important thing was that we were a family again (for the time being), and that was all that mattered. Even though Deuce and I separated yet again (surprise), we are still a family. My kids are still my kids, and they do not disrespect their mothers. All of them know better now. They all know that daddy is crazy, and he will be put his size thirteen feet in their behinds if they get out of line!

During this ordeal, I even took the liberty of calling in on a local evening radio talk show, and the host told me that I did what was needed for the situation. A large number of fathers called the show and agreed with the talk show host, and I was surprised at the number of mothers who called the show supporting me as well. It seems that parents are tired of having their hands tied by the government and are going back to the "old school" way of dealing with their kids. I am not saying that you should do what I did, but this was a personal decision that I made, and I was willing to accept the consequences.

Sometimes we as parents have to do what is right in spite of the crazy laws from our government. *You should never allow your children to hold you hostage in your own home!* If they know that they can punk you, then what is there to stop them from trying to punk someone out in the streets? Nine times out of ten, this person would hurt or maybe kill them in the streets instead of trying to chastise them. We must keep control of our homes and not let the government dictate to us about proper parenting. I am sure some of you would have handled the situation differently, and I encourage you to do what you feel is appropriate for you. There is a need for laws to protect those kids in danger, but the parents need to be protected as well. We are on our own until the bureaucratic morons come to their senses!

7 Kids Challenge # 6: Are your kids ruling your house? If your kids are disrespectful to you in the home, how do you think they act outside of the home? I challenge you to take back your power! Use whatever responsible and appropriate measures to get your children back in line. This is very important because you just may be saving their lives!

7.

DEFEATING DEPRESSION

"As long as I'm alive, I still have a chance."

ONE OF MY FAVORITE artists of all time is Vincent Van Gogh. I consider him the father of the Impressionist movement in art and a masterful genius with a brush. As great as this man was, he suffered from mental illness. Doctors for the last hundred years say that he could have suffered from bipolar disorder, schizophrenia or even syphilis. Regardless of the condition, he cut off one of his earlobes and eventually killed himself. Many years ago, I was having a serious bout with depression to the point where I was so sick of life that I walked into traffic trying to commit suicide. I'm going to tell you exactly how I got to that point and how easy it can be for all of us to temporarily give in to our weaknesses, but first let's look at this evil monster that has destroyed so many lives called Depression.

Depression can be defined in many ways, but in most cases, it is the experience of melancholy (unhappy feelings) or hopelessness as a response to high levels of stress, biochemical abnormalities, hormonal imbalances, or other causes. Endogenous depression is a type of depression that can be due to internal biochemical abnormalities. Depression can also be brought on by financial and societal situations. In my earlier discussion on teen suicide, I explained that young black men have a high rate of killing themselves because of their surroundings and environment. I was no different than any other black kid growing up, and I had my share of temptations to play Russian roulette!

Shortly after graduating from high school in 1992, I was homeless for the first time. I went into detail earlier about my second dance with homelessness when I had my daughter with me *(chapter 1)*, but this is how it all began. I left home at eighteen because my mother and I were not getting along too well. I learned quickly that being on your own is no walk in the park. I did not have my mom yelling in my ears anymore, but I was now responsible for myself. I was a young man with no job skills and no money. I walked the streets of Atlanta day and night trying to find a job and a place to lay my head. I wondered why no one would hire a dirty, smelly, long haired black kid with no experience.

I tried to get into a shelter after a couple of days of sleeping on the streets. This shelter was designed for women and children only (Remember that from chapter 1?). I seemed to find many of these shelters, and no one would let me in. I was directed to another homeless shelter and I hurried there. This place was filthy, to say the least, but it was the only place available. Grown men who had lost all hope in life surrounded me. Some were drunks; others were men who lost everything in a divorce. There were also guys who were laid off of their jobs, and a lot of the men were slowly dying from AIDS. This was a very depressing situation, and I wondered why I was there.

I got up early the next morning determined never to return to that place. I was going to find a job no matter what. In my youthful ignorance, I did not quite realize that if I found a job that day that it would not mean that I would have enough money for a place to stay immediately. Regardless, I walked and applied to every place I saw. Unfortunately, I did not find anything that day, and I became more depressed. I sat down on Peachtree Street to rest my aching feet for a while. My body was exhausted, so I decided to lie down and catch a nap. I must have been asleep for maybe ten minutes before I felt warm liquid running down my face. I opened my eyes, and it was three college kids from Georgia Tech urinating on me! *"Look at the piss poor homeless kid! Now he's piss poor for real!"* is what they were saying as they laughed. Let's just say that I got up and chased those bastards for a block before the Atlanta Police stepped in.

They said that I was trying to rob them! I explained to the officer that they urinated on me and even showed him that I was still wet! The urine was still running down my face and back! The college kids said that I pissed on myself and the officer believed them! Three rich white kids from Georgia Tech versus one poor black homeless kid from the streets in the early 90's. You do the math. I was arrested and taken to jail for attempted robbery! I was later released because another officer explained to numb-nuts that it was physically impossible for me to whip out my privates and urinate on the top of my head. I am very proud of my size down there, but I am not THAT big! I made it to a homeless shelter, cleaned myself up, and found a job within a couple of days. I worked as a janitor for some of the local fast food restaurants. I cleaned up their bathrooms and took out their trash. I was compensated with a small check and food. I kept those jobs until I finally made it off the streets.

I had conquered homelessness, but I still carried around my depression. I met Uno later that year and carried the depression into my marriage with her. I have already gone into some of the things I had to deal with in my marriage to her, so I am not going to bore you by re-emphasizing it. The bottom line is that I could not handle all the rejection from my wife and that is when I got the bright idea to kill myself by walking in traffic. Real genius I was! I was arrested again, but instead of taking me to jail, the officers took me to Grady Memorial Hospital in Atlanta.

All I could do was just weep as the officers asked me repeatedly what was wrong with me. They took me to the 13th floor where I stayed for two weeks. While I was there, I got the help I needed, and realized that I was in much better condition than some of the other people there. I was depressed, but some of these folks had more serious issues! One guy had completely lost his mind. He did not even know who he was! He said that he murdered his wife, blacked out, and never mentally recuperated! There was also a young woman there who drooled constantly and thought that she was a space explorer from Jupiter who crashed her ship here on Earth! I found out that her mother forced her into prostitution and drug abuse until her brain shut down!

These people had serious problems; I just needed to take control of my life! My dad left me, I was raped as a kid, I was homeless and urinated on, and I had an unfaithful woman, but at least I still had my mind (sort of). I got up, left that place, and never returned. I made enough money for a one way ticket to Las Vegas and opened up another dumb chapter in my life, but that story comes later *(chapter 10)*. I was back in Georgia within four months and got back in touch with my children.

Today, I still have my vicissitudes, but I do not allow myself to sink back down into that dark, dismal abyss of depression and self-destruction. I must admit that there have been times when I have lost my way, but I quickly get back on the right path and do what I have to do to keep my mind right. This has been excruciatingly hard at times. Depression is not something that just goes away; it is a daily struggle.

I have said that our kids will emulate us whether we like it or not. Sometimes they cannot help it because of heredity. I found this out by dealing with my baby boy #6. My depression had been passed to him, and he had begun to act out. He was born just two years before Uno and I had divorced. He did not get a chance to grow up with me in the house, and he did not remember me when I was there. He was jealous of his older siblings because they were able to spend a lot of time with me and even more jealous of #7 when she was born because she was living with me.

He was no longer the baby, I was not with his mother anymore, and I had a brand new wife, a new baby girl and three step-children who lived with me because Deuce was their mother. This was quite a lot for a little boy to swallow. The older he got, the more he lashed out. He started acting up in school and giving Uno a hard time. He constantly bickered with his brother and sister when he was at home and bickered with the other kids when he visited me on the weekends. I wondered what was wrong with him because in my eyes I gave him love and affection. Nobody could understand why he was always upset.

I received a phone call from his school one day. The teacher said to me that she had enough of him disturbing her class and that I needed to come pick him up. I got off work and drove across town to the school to see what was going on with my son. He was sitting in the principal's office with one of his teachers. They told me that he was a menace in the third grade, and something needed to be done about him, or he would be expelled. I looked at my son in anger at first until he started crying. I walked him out of the office and asked him what his problem was. *"I want you daddy. I'm the only kid that has never really spent any time with you. You're there for everybody else but me!"* he said as he continued to cry.

I knew that he was right. I had unknowingly ignored his needs because I was so busy taking care of Deuce and her kids along with #7. He needed some alone time with just me. All I could do was just embrace my son, tell him how important he was to me, and dedicate more of my time for just him. He felt abandoned as I did when I was his age. I never thought that I would make one of my own children feel this way, knowing how I suffered as a kid. He had become depressed with low self-esteem, hated how he looked, and believed that he was the cause of my divorce with his mother. *"You left us. It's all my fault!"* he shouted. I held my son tighter and repeatedly told him that our divorce had nothing to do with him.

This was a time when words were not enough. He needed to see some action from me. I scheduled more time off and dedicated that time to him. He had lots of love from his mother, but a father's love is vitally important to a child as well. We are responsible for their emotional stability. Many studies have proven that children with a strong father or father figure have a better chance at life and mental well-being. Fathering is more than just paying child support; it is the active hands-on relationship that gives these kids a fighting chance in this awful and cruel world. I had to learn this the hard way and both I and my son suffered for it.

I had to learn to pay attention to all of my kids as often as I could. I did this by organizing family events and scheduling alone time with all seven of them. I let them all know that they are important to me. This can be hard to do for so many children, but it is so worth it. I could not have done this if I had given in to my depression and killed myself. I am so proud that I stood firm and made it through the storm. I defeated my enemy and constantly help my son deal with his.

Depression in adults and children is equally dangerous and deadly. Longitudinal studies found that early-onset depression often persists, recurs, and continues into adulthood. Other dangerous disorders can ride "piggy-back" with depression causing a person to suffer from anxiety, disruptive behavior, substance abuse disorders, and diabetes. It is important to be able to spot depression early within you or your child. Early detection could very well save your lives!

SYMPTOMS OF DEPRESSION:

1. Constant sad or empty mood.
2. Diminished interest of pleasure in almost all activities.
3. Significant change in appetite and or body weight.
4. Difficulty sleeping or oversleeping.
5. Growing signs of agitation.
6. Fatigue or loss of energy.
7. Feelings of worthlessness or inappropriate guilt.
8. Difficult to think, concentrating and indecisive.
9. Constant thoughts of death or suicide.

If you have been diagnosed with depression but do not want to take medication for it, there are alternatives. Certain herbs and the changing of your lifestyle to more positive activities can help tremendously. Eating healthier foods with regular exercise goes a long way toward improving your self-esteem as well as your self-image. Did you know that a **deficiency in nutrients can lead to depression by altering the functions in the brain? Having the right amount of nutrients greatly influences your brain and mood.**

Taking supplements like a B-complex formula or St. John's Wort is very effective in treating mild to moderate depression. I am including a list of vitamins that provide a natural cure for mild to moderate depression along with their benefits. Please see a doctor before taking these supplements.

5-HTP

Benefits – Better mood balance, decrease in appetite (weight loss), reduced anxiety, better impulse control and better sleep.

B Vitamins

Benefits – Better mood, increased energy, and alertness, and higher learning ability, increase memory speed of thinking, verbal fluency, better concentration, increased ability to focus and higher visual clarity.

Cod Liver Oil

Benefits – Helps fight and prevent heart disease, cancer, depression, Alzheimer's, arthritis, diabetes, ulcers, hyperactivity and many other diseases. Increases your energy level and ability to concentrate. Provides greater resistance to common illnesses such as flu and cold. Helps pregnant women avoid premature births, low birth weight, and other complications.

Ginkgo Biloba

Benefits – Helps to treat: Impaired mental function in the elderly, age-related memory loss, impaired circulation in the legs, PMS symptoms, macular degeneration, sexual dysfunction due to anti-depressant medication, vertigo, dizziness, altitude sickness, tinnitus and ringing in the ears.

SAM-e

Benefits – Works faster than other antidepressants and generally makes you feel better within a week.

If you are uncomfortable with taking these supplements, there are foods that you can eat that will provide you with the same benefits. Foods rich in Serotonin, GABA, Acetylcholine, Dopamine and Norepinephrine will help to regulate the mind and ease depression. I put together a quick reference list of foods that you can eat everyday that will help.

Your Quick Reference Shopping List:

Turkey, Ham, Milk, Cheese, Carbohydrates, Brown rice, Cottage cheese, Peanuts, Sesame seeds, Mackerel, Tuna, Tilapia, Wheat Bran, Wheat Germ, Algae, Green Leafy Vegetables, Egg Yolks, Blackstrap Molasses, Fruits and vegetables with vitamins C and E, Almonds, Avocados, Bananas, Lima beans, Pumpkin seeds and Beef Liver.

If you are suffering with depression, you are not alone. People from all walks of life suffer from this disease and are fighting everyday to stay healthy. You would be surprised that many influential people have suffered from depression. Doctor Sigmund Freud, Greg Louganis, Abraham Lincoln, Terry Bradshaw, Adam Ant, Jim Carrey, Beethoven, Carrie Fisher, Johnny Depp, Kate Hudson, Rick Springfield, Uma Thurman,

Beyonce Knowles, Mandy Moore, J.K. Rowling, Marilyn Monroe, Alanis Morissette, Brooke Shields, Phil Spector, Steven Morrissey, Robert Blake, Kurt Vonnegut, Vincent van Gogh, Tipper Gore, Kelly Holmes, Tom Petty, Olivia Newton-John, Jessica Simpson, Rosie O'Donnell, Hillary Clinton, Mike Wallace, Ted Turner, Carmen Electra, Kurt Cobain, Roseanne, Jean-Claude Van Damme, Axel Rose, Carnie Wilson, Eminem, Ashley Judd, Lindsay Lohan, Amy Winehouse, Zach Braff, Britney Spears, Anna Nicole Smith.

Bet you thought depression just affected regular Joes like us, huh! Fighting depression can be a lifelong battle and is a serious disease that can be inherited from a parent. Depression has managed to affect multiple generations of my family from my great grandmother all the way down to my youngest son. I must reiterate that early detection is a vital key to defeating depression and saving the precious lives of our children as well as our own. I have battled depression for over thirty years, and some days are better than others. I still have my moments when I want to crawl into a dark corner and never come out, but I know that *as long as I'm alive, I have a chance!*

7 Kids Challenge # 7: Do you think that your child is showing signs of depression? Early detection in both adult and childhood depression is vitally important. This awful disease has claimed so many lives because of late response. I challenge you to be proactive and get help for you or your child as soon as possible. You are too important to your child's future and your child is too important to you!

8.

NO DADDY HERE

"He taught me what not to do."

I KNOW THAT I have gone over many things in this book, but I want to dive a little deeper into what really made me the man I am today. My father was very abusive to my mom and left us back in the 70's. I am not going into detail of the many issues between my mother and me after he left, but I am going to talk more about the man I call "PHANTOM." I call my father the phantom because he was never there for me, and I saw him less than 100 times in my life.

Before I go any further, I will give him his just due. He was an excellent grandfather to my children, and he took the time to love them the way a grandfather should. All of the memories my babies have of him are positive, and I will forever be grateful to him for that. I feel that this was his way of making things right because of his lack of effort with me. Regardless of his reasons, I thank him, and I am very grateful that he did it.

Conversely, my father and I never had much of a relationship. He would call to see how the kids were doing, and I would let them talk to him. When they were done and handed me back the phone, there was silence between us. We did not have anything in common. All he said was that he was proud of the man that I had become. For years, I really did not care about those words because I carried a grudge against him for leaving me. I will forever regret those feelings because now my daddy is dead.

In March of 2007, I was sitting at home and received a phone call from Uno. She was crying on the phone, and I heard my children crying in the background. I asked her what was wrong, and she told me that my father had died. My grandmother did not have my number, so she informed Uno and told her to call me. I dropped the phone as I sat back in my chair in shock. I could not believe that my father was dead. I was in denial for a few hours before it really hit me. Daddy was gone forever this time, and there was no coming back!

Deuce drove me down to Alabama to meet with my brother. After she dropped me off, she returned to Atlanta to take care of the kids. I sat down with my brother and asked what happened. He informed me that daddy was very sick and that he had lost over 90 pounds because of his illness. He told me that I would not recognize him if I saw him. He also told me that our baby brother had no emotion at all towards dad's passing. Dad had abandoned all of us, and he had an even stronger grudge against him than I. Dad was a "rolling stone" like the song says. He left my mother, married their mother, and then left her too. There was a lot of anger built up over the years, and it was starting to come out now.

We picked up baby brother and all went to dad's house to look for any paperwork he might have left. We needed to know if he had any life insurance, what bills he had, and if he had a will. Our family was not talking, so we had to do things on our own. We felt that they were hiding something from us, and we wanted to know what it was. We searched the house and noticed that our family had already gone through his important paperwork and had taken it! All we found was a bunch of expired life insurance policies. The funny thing was that on all of those policies, our grandfather was the beneficiary! Document after document, grandfather was on everything. We all looked at each other and were not surprised. Dad lived his life as if we his children did not exist! Anger swelled as we continued to look around.

My baby brother stumbled across some freaky pictures of dad and various women. It was clear Daddy was a freak as we saw him having numerous nude women posing in very erotic positions in the photos we discovered. My brothers saw pictures of their mother and quickly snatched them out of there. Thank God that there were no pictures of my mom! She was smart enough to do the nasty without the evidence! We continued to look, finding nothing but more freakiness. It seemed this man was obsessed with sex! But I can't be too quick to judge because I can never get enough sex!

Anyway, a few days passed and the funeral home called and said that daddy's body was ready to be viewed. The entire family was there, and my brothers and I pulled up. We did not know what to expect because we felt that our family might be holding back valuable information from us. We walked in, and I saw dad. He did not look like the same man that I knew as my father. My brothers and I stood there emotionless as we looked at the man who helped bring us into the world. We all held a grudge against him but remained silent out of respect. I could not cry to save my life. The tears just were not there to be shed. The other family members broke down one after the other. They were perplexed as to why we were not bothered that dad was gone. Even his friends and co-workers were clearly more emotional than we were. I just held my grandmother and comforted her while she cried.

My brothers and I were asked by the funeral home to sign the papers and be responsible for the funeral cost. We found it funny that the man who did nothing for us needed us to pay for his funeral! We signed the papers and walked out of the office. Isn't it ironic that some people can go their entire lives without thinking of you, and in death there is only you there thinking of them? We got outside, the family was loading into their cars, and my cousin and I got into an argument. She wanted to know why we were snooping around trying to gather information about our dad! She said that she had done all the work for us, and we needed to just trust her. Well, one thing led to another and it escalated into an all-out shouting match. I said that we had every right to check up behind her, and if she was not hiding anything, she should not be this upset. She tossed a few curse words at me, and I tossed them back as if we were playing bad word tennis!

My uncle then grabbed me and told me that I should respect her and shut-up! I did not appreciate his putting his hands on me, but I was not going to beat the old man down. I still had respect for him, so I decided to cool off and let it go. He released me and they all left. I was highly upset, but it was not worth the Birmingham police arresting me for beating down an old man in front of a funeral home!

I went to my aunt's (my mom's sister) house to get away from my daddy's people. She lived across town, and it was just what I needed at the time. I needed a break from all the drama and a good meal in my stomach to help me rest. While I was at my aunt's house, we talked a lot about my mom and her past as a child. My aunt told me things that my mom would never have told me. I wish to hell that she had because this was information that would have helped me to better understand my mom and not hate her. My aunt also got into some of the history between my mom and dad when I was a child. My dad was no saint, and he really did not care if everyone knew it! I am not going to get into details, but I truly understand now why mom lost her mind every time I mentioned his name.

Later that night, Uno, #4, #5, #6 and my mom pulled up into the driveway. They were here for the funeral and to give me support in this rough time. I hugged Uno and the kids, sat down with mom, and had the talk that took thirty years to have. My mother finally told me some things about my father and his family that made my mouth drop to the floor. There are so many things that we do not understand as children, and when our eyes are opened as adults, we realize just how stupid we were in our youth! I apologized for everything that I did out of ignorance to my mother. I told her that I did not agree with how she handled many things but that I understood why she had such hatred in her heart to-wards my father.

I managed to talk to my brother's mother also. She reiterated many of the things that my mom was talking about. Apparently, dad did her the same way and even took it steps further so that she had to ultimately leave him as well. All of the things that these two women were telling me were shocking but strangely familiar to me. I can be mad all day long for what my dad did to my mom, but I did some of the same foolishness with my own two wives! The man did not raise me, but there where times when I acted just like him! I was my father's son in more ways than one! I was humiliated and ashamed and humbled myself in front of my mother.

The next day was the funeral, and I put on one of my father's suits to so-called honor him. There was malice and ill intent in my heart as I put it on. I was to speak at the funeral, and I was determined to tell the unmitigated truth about the man I called dad. I was going to expose him for the low-down scumbag that he was in his own suit, in front of his family, in his church! My mother told me to hold my peace and do the honorable thing because he was dead, and there was no point to it. My aunt, Uno, Deuce and my brother's mom all told me the same thing. I had hate and anger spewing from my veins, and I could not wait to roast him in front of everybody! I strongly disagreed with them all the way to the point when it was time to express myself in front of a crowd of his peers. I was going to light him up so bad that I would not be surprised if Dad rose from that coffin and looked me in the face!

I stepped behind the pulpit and addressed the church. I scanned the crowd and saw all of my father's family members in the front pews. I scanned the crowd again and saw Deuce with #1, #2, #3, and #7. I saw Uno with the other children, and I saw mom in the back of the church. They all had that same look on their faces. They did not want me to degrade this man at his own funeral! After I initially spoke to the congregation, I paused briefly. After a few deep breaths, I mentioned how wonderful a grandfather my dad was to my children. A huge sigh of relief came from everybody who knew my intent as I concentrated on the positives and took the high road. The important thing is that he treated my children like gold, and there was no need in demonizing him in their eyes. All they knew was that he was the best granddaddy in the world, and it would not be fair for me to destroy that image for them.

I closed my comments by thanking my cousin with whom I had argued the day before. She had done such a wonderful job on the funeral arrangements, and she deserved to be praised for her effort. I thanked my grandmother for being such a rock of foundation for me. Then I thanked my mother. I gave her the validation that she needed in front of the people that she had been warring with for over thirty years! I finally knew the truth, but I will let the truth die with my dad.

We laid Dad to rest at the cemetery, and I watched as they loaded his body into the mausoleum. The sound of the coffin scraping against the cement was too much for me to handle. I finally broke down and cried myself sick! Regardless of all the things that he had done, he still was my father. I could not contain the pain and grief any longer. The reality that he was gone had finally hit me like a ton of bricks! I did not realize how much I loved the man until that moment. Deuce comforted me as I shed an ocean of tears that I had held back for so many years. It was then when I truly realized that life is too short, and that I must love my children as hard as I can for as long as I can!

We must not live our lives in secret and negativity because when the time comes, our children may tell the ugly truth about us after we are dead! I have a much greater appreciation for my mother and my dad. I understand that relationships can go very wrong at times, and no one is perfect. The only thing you can do is do better next time and fix what once was so broken and break the cycle of wrongdoings so that your kids will not have to clean up your mess!

This is the poem that I wrote as a tribute to my father as it appeared on the program of his funeral.

THE SUN

By

A PROUD SON

When I was a child, I met a man...

He was a giant of a man to me...

He stood as tall as a building...

His shoulders were as wide as the sky...

And his voice thundered when he spoke...

He would pick me up with his strong arms and lift me to the heavens...

And gently bring me back down to earth, longing to go again...

There was magic in his eyes, as he always knew the answers to my questions...

The great mystery of this man baffled me because he knew me more than I knew myself...

I felt at ease as I looked into his face as if I were looking into a mirror...

The miracle of me seeing my future, and him seeing his past, all in this present time...

As I grew, I no longer saw him as a building but instead he became more of a large hill that I could look over...

It seems that over time he deliberately shrunk in size to make me feel better...

I could look down upon his head and rub it sometimes because there was no hair…

The giant building had become a man to me, but oh what an amazing man, as the large hill became a roadway pointing me in the right direction…

I make my way down the road and eventually find my place as I look down and see my children looking up with smiles on their faces gazing at the giant building that I had become…

The building…the hill…the man…is my father…

He has risen into the sky and become the sun that will always shine down on me.

Most people who knew my dad say that my brothers and I sent him off to the next world from his funeral better than he deserved through my speech, my poem and the eloquent words my brother spoke about him as well. I disagree with the way my father left me high and dry when I was a child, and he definitely taught me everything "NOT" to do, but I have learned to let it all go and appreciate the good that was in him. I am determined to be a much better dad and man than he ever was. I said it, and I am done with it.

7 KIDS Challenge # 8: Are you an absentee father? I challenge all absentee fathers to stop reading this book now and get in touch with your kids and schedule time with them within the next 10 days.

9.

WHY DO I ACT THE WAY I DO?

*"Whatever you are accustomed to is what
you will desire psychologically."*

IF YOU WANT OUT...THEN OPEN THE DOOR AND LEAVE!
I know that this can be hard at times, but it can be done! I think that I
have done a very good job changing my life around. Nevertheless, what is
the point in telling you that without showing you how I did it? In order
for me to change and open those doors, I had to figure out how things
worked. I discovered that I was addicted to drama. I had experienced
negativity all of my life, so I was drawn to negative people in order to keep
recreating more of the same. I do not claim to be a psychiatrist, and I am
not going to bore you with medical jargon; however, I will try my best to
explain this in nonprofessional, REAL WORLD terms.

To put it plainly, if you grew up around domestic violence and abuse,
there is a good chance that you will continue this behavior into your
adulthood. The human body has a natural tendency to maintain ho-

meostasis. According to the 'Oxford Colour Medical Dictionary, Third Edition' (paraphrasing) **Homeostasis** is the way living organisms regulate their internal environment to maintain a stable, constant condition through a process called **down regulation.** Down regulation is conditioned through life experience. If a behavior consistently occurs in the same environment, the brain will adjust to the presence of the conditioned cues by decreasing the number of available receptors in the absence of the behavior. In simple terms, **whatever you are accustomed to is what you will desire psychologically.** Your brain is the key to unlock your cure! I know this is true because I experienced it myself.

Our brains are super computers that are programmed through software (emotions), and our software is constantly updated through life experience. When we are born, we have an empty hard drive that soaks up information like a sponge. We gather this information and turn it into associative behavior. Our belief structure and the way we view ourselves is downloaded from our parents and surrounding environment.

Patterns of behavior and thought are constantly hitting our system as "pop-up" ads. Through time, we click on the ones that are desirable and discard the others. Just like in computers, pop-up ads can carry viruses that are designed to hurt, manipulate or cause our computers (brains) to shutdown. They are harmful and can take a lot of work to remove; it is even more work to fix the damage. Life experience can be the mother of all pop-up ads that influences our emotions; our experiences either leave our brains in a good state of mind or destined to crash and burn!

Each emotion produces its own chemical that is released and sent through your system. In cases of dependence and withdrawal, the body has become so dependent on high concentrations of the particular chemical stemming from a frequent emotion (for example, depression) that it has stopped producing other chemicals in order to maintain homeostasis. The production of "happy chemicals" is shut down because the brain is not used to being happy! It has been bombarded with depression over a long period of time, so it will aggressively protect itself from change. This is simple logic; the more you are depressed, the more you will be depressed!

Ending a particular pattern of thought can be extremely difficult at times. These thoughts are linked to some very traumatic times in your life and not forgotten easily. In my case, I was raped at camp, and I still remember it to this day. That experience latched on to other previous negative experiences and kept me in a depressive state of mind through homeostasis.

It is so easy for me to remember all the bad things that have happened to me in vivid detail, but I can barely remember when my children were born! I know that I was there, but I could not tell you any vivid details. My brain simply shut it out because it was a happy thought and not depressing. Those memories directly challenged what my brain was accustomed to, so it eliminated the threat by storing those happy memories away in some dark place of no remembrance!

I had to challenge my brain to reboot those happy thoughts by forcing myself to be happy! I started treating myself better. I went to the movies more often. I ate at some restaurants where I always wanted to eat. I started flirting with women just to do it. I started to see the joy that I brought to my children when they saw me. I even bought a puppy! These minor steps had a great impact in my life. I had to constantly do happy things for a long period to reprogram my brain. I actually spoiled myself for a change! The happier I was, the happier I wanted to be!

This changed my entire outlook on life and eventually changed my behavior through my changed mind. I had become a positive person with people wanting to be around me instead of a dark, depressed tyrant whom everybody scorned! I learned that if I want happiness around me, then I must spread happiness to others. I was much nicer to Uno and Deuce for a long period, and they gradually saw the change.

The most important thing is that the change is permanent and not temporary. My brain is now more accustomed and attuned to being happy, so my brain will aggressively protect this state of mind. I had to trick my brain to use homeostasis for the good instead of the bad! Below is a list of the different modes of addiction and their possible cures from Rankin, J.G., Etiology, Vol. 8 of Core Knowledge in the Drug Field. Ottawa: Non-medical use of Drugs Directorate, National Health and Welfare, 1978.

Moral Model

This model of addiction is based on a moralistic system of behavior or what is right and wrong. It is believed that moral addictions are defects of character resulting from human weaknesses and negative impulses. It implements religious measures of moral behavior by damning those who choose to operate in a sinful manner. People who are addicted to drugs and alcohol are considered evil and lack the moral strength to overcome their adversity through lack of faith. It is said that according to this model, the only treatment for people suffering from moral addiction is to punish them by locking them up in jail. These people are considered to be bad and should be banished from society.

My point of view:

The last time I checked, the only perfect person on the Earth died over two thousand years ago. He was killed for being perfect! We all have moral weaknesses in us. This is why some of us fall into this mode of addiction so easily. If this describes you, then you really need to do some soul searching and figure out what really makes you happy spiritually and stick to it. No minister, preacher or prophet can give to you what you can give to yourself. Only you know what spiritually makes you happy and what helps you to make the correct moral decisions for yourself. Find your path, and walk it with passion! I consider this mode to be barbaric and out dated. Like the old saying goes, "He who has no sin cast the first stone!"

Biological/Disease Models

This particular model of addiction assumes that people addicted to alcohol or drugs suffer from a physical defect that causes their addiction. Similar to the moral model, these people are supposedly screwed up. The difference is that they are not bad people but unfortunate enough to develop their addiction biologically through no fault of their own. It is believed that there is no cure for this form of genetic addiction. The only treatment is abstinence, which may drive the addiction into remission. They may have inherited their addiction from their parents or someone in their bloodline as a type of generational curse like the addictions to depression in my family.

My point of view:

My mother suffered from depression addiction, and she passed it along to me; then I passed it on to my youngest son. Because my mother had an awful past (at no fault of her own) she sometimes created a carbon copy of that environment from her childhood for me to grow up in, resulting in my own issues of depression. In order for me to break the chain of this awful disease, I had no choice but to change for my kids' sake and my own! I did not want them to have the life that I had, so I did what was necessary to prevent that awful future for them and generations to come. This stuff is serious and real! If you want it to stop, then make it stop! The great thing about this model of addiction is that ONE person CAN change it, and that person's actions will affect generations! Are you the one to change it, or is your child going to have to do it for you?

Sociological Models

It seems that society is obsessed with celebrity worship. This includes film and television stars, music artists, and popular athletes. Trying to emulate the fantasy world of Hollywood celebrities can be a daunting task, but that never stopped anyone from trying! Everyone wants to know what is going on in Hollywood, and even worse, they want to be like Hollywood! The Sociological Model of Addiction suggests that societies that produce higher levels of conflict, suppressed aggression, stress, and sexual tensions are at a high risk of alcohol and drug use.

As a matter of fact, in these societies the more booze and drugs you consume, the more popularity you gain, and you earn your stripes as a party animal and socialite. Sounds like Hollywood to me! Peer pressure is a major contributor to this model of addiction. The addicts believe that the abuse of alcohol and drugs can be used to reduce anxiety and provide an escape from their problems. Manufacturers of alcohol and tobacco market their products in a manner that feeds into this addiction through commercials on television, the movie screen, and at major sporting events.

My point of view:

It has been suggested that the only cure for this model of addiction is to change the world and make it a better place where there is no more alcohol and drugs on the streets. Well, good luck with that. Changing the world can be a tedious process, and quite frankly, you may not live long enough to see it. So how about taking an inward approach and concentrating on changing yourself and the people you hang with? This is so much easier than trying to be Jesus, Joan of Ark, JFK or MLK. They were all killed for their efforts!

Psychological/Social Learning Models

These models state that excessive alcohol and drug use are problem behaviors that are learned in response to certain people, places, things, events, thoughts, and feelings. It pretty much states that some people abuse alcohol and drugs simply because of how they make them feel. They want to get high or intoxicated and feel the effect of the drugs moving through their system. The drugs have a psychological effect on the mind and how it responds when stimulated while under the influence.

Euphoria is reached in the mind as well as the body. The addict becomes addicted to that feeling to the point where they crave for that feeling constantly. If they do not give in to their temptation, the body may respond by shutting down and going through withdrawal. These addicts are not considered to be bad people but are viewed as victims of a powerful substance that can take over and dominate anyone because of the influence it has over the human mind and body.

My point of view:

When I was in college, I must say that I got high a few times, and it felt good! I was experimenting and wanted to see what all the hoopla was about. I felt that I was floating on clouds and could kiss an angel's ass if I wanted to! After I came down, I suffered a massive headache that would not go away. I thought that my head was going to explode and everyone would know that I was getting high in my apartment! Let's just say that I don't do drugs anymore because my body cannot take it.

I didn't develop some enormous inner strength to fight off the craving; I was just too scared of dying to try them again! For those whose immune system is much stronger than mine who are addicted under this model, you must learn new ways and healthy behaviors that can give you that same "high" feeling in place of the drugs and booze. You have to actually want to change in order for this process to work!

You can take all the pills you want and go to all the programs, but nothing will change until you change! Addiction in any form can be destroyed through an assertive effort. There is nothing mystical or magical about this. There is no need to walk on water. All you need is the drive to make the decision to finally take control of your life!

I came to a conclusion that to have the type of life that I always wanted, I had to change my life! No more quick temper, self-destructive behavior, or addiction! I had to be done with all the hurt of my childhood, failed marriages and allowing people to dictate my mood and responses! I ultimately learned how to rule myself and always look for the path of the positive in any situation that would advance me and not hurt me without artificial substances.

This took many years to master, and I endured what seemed like an eternity of unnecessary drama with plenty of knots on my head from banging it on the proverbial wall! This is not a quick fix by any means, and I don't want anyone thinking that their problems will magically go away after reading this book and going cold turkey from their addiction. I encourage you to seek professional counseling if necessary, go to church more often if you have to, but always see yourself as the man that you want to be and not the man that you are. Fix the man in the mirror gradually, and be patient until you get your breakthrough.

7 Kids Challenge # 9: Are you suffering from "Bad Homeostasis"? I challenge you to aggressively seek out happiness. Focus on healthy and positive transitions for a changed life through your changed mind. Do not be tempted to fall back into the same old rut. Positive change is HARD, but you owe it to yourself to try!

10.

TURNING PAIN INTO PROFIT!

"You can fail a million times, but just succeed once, and your life will change forever!"

MY LIFE HAS MOST certainly been very interesting to say the least. It seemed that everywhere I turned; there was a new dark chapter of my life about to open up another can of whoop-ass on me! I used to always shout aloud, *"How much can a man take?! God, do you hate me?!"* For years, I felt that God had a grudge against me. I got raped as a kid, just to grow up and have the same things happen to me emotionally as an adult. I wondered what I did to tick God off!

In life, things just have a way of happening whether you deserve it or not. Instead of wasting my time with the woe as me attitude and throwing my own pity parties, I should have realized that awful things happen to teach valuable lessons for the future. These dubious events helped to mold and structure my life into a life of purpose and strength. I have a lot in common with just about everyone that approaches me for advice. If I do not understand what you are going through, then you are not from Earth!

I look back at my life and see an entire laundry list of failures and disappointments. There is one thing that I have learned over the years that gives me hope. *You can fail a million times, but just succeed once, and your life will change forever!* The perfect models for this are Bill Gates (one of the richest men in the world), Thomas Edison (inventor of the light bulb) and Hank Aaron (major league baseball legend). These men started off just like you and me with a simple dream. The difference between these great men and the average Joe is that they all had a decisive "plan of action" to achieve their goals.

We all have dreams, but very few of us have the gonads to develop a plan and aggressively go after those dreams! It seems that people are afraid of success and are too lazy to work for what they want out of life. Some may strive for success, but they allow their loved ones to talk them out of their dreams and listen to garbage like this: *"Oh, you can't do that. It will never work!"* It is easier to spend a lifetime complaining about your dead-end job, how much you hate your boss, the crappy car you drive, your spouse getting fat, how much you hate the rich and your so-called under achieving life! This kind of thinking is insane!

Thomas Edison –

In the days of Edison, no one could conceive an artificial light source that was powered by electricity. The use of burning wax candles and torches for light could never become obsolete; this is what people thought because that is all they knew. One man was not comfortable with the old traditional approach and chose to think outside the box and come up with something innovative and better than what was available.

People who think this way are not considered normal! Most successful millionaires and billionaires are not normal; this is a good thing! People thought that Edison was a nut case because he failed over 10,000 times. Despite the criticism, he pushed through and finally invented something that would change the world! This planet will be forever grateful for his wonderful mind. As for all of his doubters, they are rotting away in a grave forgotten by everyone. Who would you rather be?

Hank Aaron –

In Hank Aaron's youth, Barack Obama was not the president of the United States, and being a black man was not very popular. Things we take for granted today like drinking from any water fountain, using any restroom, or simply enjoying a meal at any restaurant were luxuries that were not given to blacks simply because of skin tone. Hank Aaron's war of wills was psychological as well as physical in a segregated and racist America. It had to be a tremendous adjustment to be cheered in a stadium full of people during the game but be mistreated by the same people outside of the baseball park! His fortitude was unyielding as he crushed the competition and even received death threats for breaking Babe Ruth's home run record. It is a shame that he could not celebrate this incredible achievement because of racism.

Mr. Aaron did not allow his circumstances, his environment, or the people around him to steer him away from his passion for the game of baseball and his dreams of success in the league. If you want to look at some of his failures, he struck out more frequently than he hit home runs, but he never gave up! It is amazing that the world of baseball mocked him in the beginning, and now he is idolized and worshiped. As for all of his doubters, they are washed up "has beens" or "never could be's" who never made it to the hall of fame and have been forgotten by everyone. Who would you rather be?

Bill Gates – Billionaire Computer Mogul

Mr. Gates did not succeed at everything that he set his mind to. He was just some young, geeky nerd trying to find his way in the world. He managed to do something right for a geek. He invested in an idea that has blossomed into the huge powerhouse Microsoft! He failed at so many things, but he definitely got this one right! As for all of his doubters, they are wishing that they had invested in that tiny company back then and become multi-millionaires many times over! Instead, they are still in the "rat race" praying that they can survive on their pensions and are forgotten by everyone. Who would you rather be?

Speaking of failures and getting things wrong, I'll let you in on some of my failed attempts at success. After getting myself off the streets the first time (*chapter 7*), I took a trip out west and landed in Las Vegas. I was just a poor kid who was looking for something to get into. The first thing I noticed is how beautiful the women were in Sin City. My mind was in the gutter all the time as I had quick thoughts of having sex with every woman who walked past me. There was something else I noticed about all these beautiful girls; they all were with rich guys who could afford to buy them anything they wanted. I was broke, and there was no way I would even have a ghost of a chance at hitting some high-dollar punnany like that! I'm not being misogynistic, I'm just being real! This is how most men think!

I had to do something if I wanted the fancy cars and gorgeous women drooling over me like I was the last man on earth. Then I had to decide if I was willing to break the law or not. Let me tell you that some decisions are easier to make than others, but when you are young, dumb, and hungry with big dreams, those decisions seem to make themselves!

I became a collector for a local loan shark, who will remain nameless. He had a list of accounts that were overdue, and he wanted his money from these poor saps who were crazy enough to borrow from him. I'm not going to go into too many details or incriminate myself, but there was one account that I will never forget. The "shark" sent me and a constituent of mine to a house in one of the Vegas suburbs to collect a substantial sum from this washed-up lawyer who was going through a divorce. His wife had cleaned him out and left him, but that was his problem, not ours. The shark wanted his money, and that's all that mattered.

I kicked the door in, and we found him in a drunken stupor passed out on the floor holding an empty bottle of Jack Daniels with drool pouring from his mouth. I pushed him around a bit to wake him up and demanded the money that was due. This poor guy just cried as he told us he didn't have the money and that his wife took it along with everything else he loved. My partner snatched the guy away from me and dragged him into a bedroom kicking and screaming.

At that moment, something told me to get out of that house and never come back. This was not the life that I had envisioned for myself. I had money and all the women that I could screw, but this was not right. I told my partner that I was leaving. After a brief argument, we both walked out of there. The man was still depressed and crying, but he was alive, and that's all that mattered! I can't go into further details, but let's just say that I left town with my life and nothing else.

I made it back to Atlanta, and even though I knew I had made the right decision, I still missed that lifestyle of having money and my pick of any woman. I went to a strip club to blow off some steam and saw all the lovely ladies sliding up and down the pole. I saw all the money that men were throwing at them and reminisced about my having money like that to just throw away. One of the strippers came to me and asked if I wanted a lap dance. I told her that I could not afford it, but I was willing to do a work trade. She had a puzzled look on her face as I told her to sit down and I danced for her! I took off my shirt and grinded on her until the song went off. I managed to attract a lot of attention as other dancers flocked toward me wanting to see the show.

After I was done and collected a half dozen numbers from the dancers, the stripper gave me twenty bucks for the lap dance. She told me that I was cute and had a body to die for and that I could make some serious money being a male stripper. She asked me if I had a stage name, and I said no. She said that I was dark as night, and I could dance up a storm. Then she said, "NYGHTSTORM! That's your name!"

I found this an interesting coincidence because I was called NYGHT-STORM a few years back when I was the first drum major for my high school marching band. I had teenage girls and grown women falling out of the stands as I high stepped and grinded on the fifty yard line during our half time shows at the football games! Let's just say that the P.T.A was not happy with my near xxx rated performances, but the principal loved how the band as a whole filled the seats and made money for the school. I guess cash overrules ethics every single time!

I stripped for a while making some great cash and banging married women. Let me state that I am in no way advocating the banging of married women. I do believe that what goes around comes back around, and in my case it did so many times in dealing with Uno and Deuce. But as a young man, the power was intoxicating as I was having passionate sex with women who owned companies and were up to twenty years my senior.

Multi-Million dollar mansions and expensive bottles of wine were the norm, and I could not believe that I was being paid to do it! I was truly enjoying the life until I was on stage one day doing a show and my mom showed up with her friends! I was so embarrassed that my mom saw me shaking my money-maker in a g-string that I got out of the business and concentrated on making an honest buck without the danger of angry husbands trying to kill me!

I call another failure of mine the *Great Music Production Fiasco*. In 1999, I started my own music production business with a few friends. None of us had any idea how to run a business, and some of my friends were too into selling drugs and prostitution to care. I tried to keep things afloat and managed to meet some very influential music people in Atlanta. They told me my music was very good and that I would be a big star as a rapper and producer.

I would love to say that the music business is such a wonderful thing, but I would be lying through my teeth! That business is just as corrupt as politics! They were not interested in me; they just wanted my material. They sold me a pipe dream, and I fell for it! I signed a contract locking me down for two years; furthermore, anything that I had produced would solely belong to them. I signed away my rights, which resulted in a major crash and burn! I still hear versions of my songs being performed by some of the biggest talent in the business today, and there is nothing that I can do about it!

Years later, after I was free of that contract and struck out on my own. I signed a young rap group out of Decatur, Georgia to my production company. I produced an album for them and had managed to find some investors to help me with their project. These guys were burning up the streets with their insanely good lyrics and my killer beats. I even started to make a name for myself when a strong independent label interested in the group approached me. This label was willing to work with me and told me that they could invest into the project. This was serious business, and the rep wanted to see them perform. I told him that the group would be performing at a certain club, and he was invited to come check them out that night.

Later that evening, I informed the group of the good news, and they were ecstatic! The major investor would be at the club waiting to see them perform. I felt that all of my dreams were about to come true! We got to the club that night, and everything was ready for the group to perform. They walked toward the stage and got into an argument with another rap group. Apparently, somebody stepped on someone's shoes, and a fight broke out! The brawl escalated and made its way outside to the street. Guns were pulled out, and people were shot at! Police swooped in quickly and arrested everyone that was involved. I saw my potential multi-million dollar rap group hauled away by the cops over a pair of sneakers!

I did not have the money to bail them out, so I approached the investor. He sternly informed me that he would not invest his hard-earned money in a bunch of thugs who were not ready for stardom! He further scolded me and told me that he was not interested in investing in a bunch of problems! He needed serious artists who were serious about their careers and rappers who knew how to keep their "thugin" in the music and not in the streets! He was right. How could we make money on a brand new group if they were always locked up? It's just not good business. My other investors pulled out as well. It took an awful long time to pay them back their money. Let's just say that these were not the type of people that you did not pay back, ok? Lesson learned!

Real estate is another one of my many ventures. I got my real estate license while I was an overnight security guard at a major hospital in Atlanta. I felt good about the accomplishment but did not realize how much work and effort goes into being an agent. Real estate is a tricky business and you had better know what you are doing, or you will fail! Let's just say that I didn't make the grade.

After being a real estate agent, I tried my hand as a home inspector. This did not go too well either. I was on a call at a particular home in North West Atlanta. This was my very first house that I was going to inspect, and I was excited. I got to the home, and I started with the crawl space. These places are not fun to get into, and you never know what is down in that dark dungeon under a house. I crawled my big butt down into the crawl space and turned on my trusty flashlight. It was dark, damp, and smelly, and I just wanted to hurry up and finish. I made my way further in, and I noticed something large moving toward me from the far right corner.

I shined my flashlight over there, and it was a huge snake! It hissed aggressively and struck at me! I screamed in terror as I quickly got out of there! The owner of the house heard my screams and came running out. I told him about the snake, and he said that it belonged to his son. *"The damn thing must have gotten out somehow,"* he said as I looked at him. I said, *"A nine foot long boa constrictor gets loose, and you don't know? I could have been killed, you bastard!*" I finished my sentence as I got back in my car and sped off. That was the first and last day I spent as a home inspector! I still sent him the bill, but I have not heard from him yet.

I told you earlier that I was a pizza deliveryman for a while (**chapter 6**). After hearing about the death of my dad (**chapter 8**), I took a leave of absence to deal with that situation. When I got back to Atlanta, I returned to work to try to get my mind off my dad's passing. There is an old saying, "*When it rains it pours.*" I pulled up in front of a house in a nice subdivision, and I saw a young man around seventeen talking on a cordless house telephone.

I noticed that the house was vacant. Before I could pull off the young man approached my car. I asked did he order the pizza. He responded by saying yeah. However, there was a problem. He said that his family had just bought the house and that they were on their way with the furniture and the money for the pizza. At that point, a second young man came running from behind the house with a pistol! They demanded the pizza and the money that I had on me. I am not intimidated by any man, but I sure as hell know that I cannot stop a bullet! I gave them what they asked for and they took off running.

I watched these two thugs run away and noticed that the first one dropped the phone that he had in his hands. I quickly grabbed the phone, hopped back in my car and drove out of there immediately! I called 911 when I got to a safe distance. The police showed up quickly and I gave the officers the dropped phone. They ran the phone number of the house phone through their database and said that the house was in the same subdivision. More units showed up and a helicopter flew high over our heads. They stormed the house and dragged them out kicking and screaming!

The idiots were eating the pizza with their friends and bragging about how they had robbed this big pizza man. All of their mothers showed up soon after, and I saw these so-called gangsters turn into little crying babies as their mothers told the cops to take them away! Those ladies were tired of their sons causing problems in the subdivision and were happy to see them on their way to jail. These kids were not poor. They all had big screen televisions in their rooms with computers, video games, everything a kid could ask for!

They were a bunch of spoiled brats who finally were getting what they deserved. I was just happy that it ended positively and that no one was hurt. I later learned that some of those kids actually turned their lives around for the better, so good for them! But as for the situation itself, there is no way in the world that I wanted to die over some pizza! I quit that job and refocused my attention to what my true calling is… writing!

I have worked many jobs, and I have been just about everything there is in the work force. I was a job coach where I helped adults with mental disorders find and keep jobs (that's ironic). I was a day laborer working alongside homeless people for $40.00 dollars a day. This was an interesting job because the regular workers on these construction sites knew that most of the day laborers were homeless and treated us like it! I have been an actor, a model, and now I am a community activist and author. It is amazing how life can take you on a journey full of twists and turns before you finally get to where you are going. I have failed at just about everything that I have touched.

My finances, my careers, and my relationships all failed until I decided to take control of my life and rise above my adversity. You must know that regardless of your difficulties, you are destined for happiness, but it is up to you to get it. How bad do you want it? What are you willing to do to get it? When you can answer those two questions, then you will be ready to be your own boss and write your own paychecks! I turned my pain into profit, and I have not looked back since! This is how I did it.

1. I first had to own my failures, admit that I was not the man that I wanted to be, and acknowledge that I needed help! There is no great success if you cannot feed yourself. I applied for government assistance in the form of food stamps, Disability (for my severe depression and PTSD) and Medicaid. There is no shame in getting the help you need. Your tax dollars from every pay check that you have earned have gone towards these programs. I took full advantage of those programs and let some of that money keep my head above water while I continued to look for a stable income. This was extremely hard, and I failed numerous times because of my severe depression, but I did not give up. Remember, this will not happen overnight! You must be persistent whether you feel like it or not!

2. Once there was money coming in (not very much but stable), I decided to change my life by changing my behavior and my overall view of myself. A good self-critique is mandatory for success! You must know thyself in order to improve thyself! Find all your faults, failures, shortcomings, and vices that are negative and be willing to go through the painful process

of detoxing from them. Learn how to amplify your good characteristics and focus on building them up. I did this by asking my ex-wives and loved ones who are close to me to tell me about myself. They wrote down my pros and cons, and I made a list of my own and analyzed them. I compared how I saw myself to how my loved ones saw me and developed a strategy to fix my weaknesses. This may take time, but the reward of having the type of life you dream of is worth it!

3. I developed a plan of action. This included deciding to write a book about my life, and learning about public speaking and marketing (self promotion). This step is very important because I had to surround myself with the type of people I wanted to be like. No one ever makes it on his or her own, and I am no exception. I put myself in the right circles and made sure to be at the right places at the right times. I prepared to represent myself when the opportunity presented itself because eventually lady luck will find you. You may only have one chance, so I wanted to make it count!

4. I made notes and wrote down everything that has happened to me, good and bad. Great stories consist of tragedy, adversity and then finally triumph. People are drawn to folks who have experienced pain and found a way to survive. This gives them hope in their lives, and they will seek you out for advice. I had plenty of advice to give because of my multiple waves of awful experiences.

5. I organized my notes and ideas into book form.

6. I hired a professional that I trusted to read and edit my work. She was worth every penny!

7. I did my homework by reading books by authors who may have a similar story or message. I saw how they broke their story down and imitated the technique. I did not try to re-invent the wheel!

8. I decided I would get my story published, no matter what I had to do! Rejection is often a part of any new writer's journey, but I pressed on! I sent out query letters to just about every literary agent I thought would be interested in my project. Most said "No way in hell! The Self-Help industry is not designed for people with your ethnic background." Knowing that I am a survivor of an awful past gave me the strength to ignore this bigot. His ignorance fueled me to invest in myself and publish my own book. I created a website to be a platform for me to promote myself and took advantage of all the FREE advertising on the web through social networks and Youtube.

9. I learned how to be open, honest, and willing to talk to people about my trials and tribulations. People are lied to all day long by their bosses, politicians and maybe their religious leaders. I saw that it was refreshing for them to find someone with valuable information they need without the cloak of deceit. People listen and support people who have things in common with them. I learned to find the common ground and tell my story, knowing that I am an expert at my own adversity. I had no idea that somehow in this crazy,

mixed up world, that my suffering and pain would help so many people learn how to successfully deal with their own.

10. And finally, I chose to write my book myself because only I can truly tell my story. I do not use ghostwriters because you do not have to be a rocket scientist to tell your own story. I have seen that some people use them and that is their choice. Ultimately, I know that as long as people can see themselves in my life experiences and draw strength to deal with their own issues, I have a real shot at long term success. Making a living helping others overcome their pain is a blessing that I will never take for granted!

7 Kids Challenge # 10: Do you still have aspirations that you have not accomplished? Time waits for no one and life is short. I challenge you to take the risk of accomplishing everything you want to do in life. No day is guaranteed, so live as if you know that you will die tomorrow. It is impossible to do everything in a short amount of time, but I want you to try! Do not take your last breath from this life full of regret!

11.

DEATH HAS NO DOMAIN

DEUCE AND I REMARRIED in January of 2008 (big surprise, huh) and we were celebrating a relationship that has stood the test of time. We were not aware of the turmoil that was coming our way. Three weeks after our wedding, we received a call from our oldest daughter (# 2) that our oldest son Victor (# 1) had been in an accident at work. He worked for a major airline at Hartsfield Jackson International Airport in Atlanta on the ramp, and we were concerned. We immediately gathered #3 and little #7 up and sped down the highway to the hospital. We got to the hospital and met up with Deuce's first husband and his wife. They were also concerned as we made our way to the emergency room.

We all sat there and waited before we were informed that he was not there but was transported to another hospital closer to the airport. We were all angry because we were originally told that he was at this hospital and were not updated until we arrived. Precious time was wasted because we were sent to the wrong hospital. We got ourselves together and sped off to the hospital where our boy was. We got there and the nurse asked us all to go into a family room and wait for the doctor. Deuce held my hand as we could only pray that our son was okay. The doctor came in and said that Victor was hit by a truck on the ramp and died. Deuce and the rest of the family cried in agony as I stood there in total shock. I refused to believe that my son was gone.

Deuce stood to her feet and said that she wanted to see him. The nurse took us back, and we saw him. The truth was too much to bear. I cannot go into any further details out of respect for my son and my family. All I wanted to know is why God decided to take my boy away. Representatives from the airport and his company showed up to lend their support for us, but I wanted answers. I wanted to know who was responsible and I wanted blood! No one knew why this happened, and they could not tell me how. All that was said is that a thorough investigation was being conducted and that we would be notified. With all of this sudden anguish, we all had to pull ourselves together to plan his funeral and lay him to rest.

After Victor's death, I must have read all the pamphlets and a ton of books on dealing with the loss of a child. I will tell you the truth when I say this; all of that wonderful information did not make me feel better at first. I had to go through the grieving process on my own and work my way through it. This was an extraordinary task because I had to be the strong one in front of my family while crying out my pain in secret when I was alone. There was so much pinned up rage in me as to why this happened. Why did my child have to die?! Why was he taken from us?! And why was I powerless to stop it?!

I distinctively remember for years joking around with my children and telling them that *"You guys are going to have to bury me one day; so I hope to God that you can get along long enough to put me in the ground."* I said this because they argued all the time amongst each other. I knew deep down they loved one another, and if someone was stupid enough to mess with one, they would have to deal with them all!

Once the common threat was gone, they would go back to their routine and tease each other. My kids have had a unique childhood because there are five adults raising them instead of just two. Let me recap; there are Deuce and me, Uno and Deuce's first husband (the father of my three step-kids) along with his wife. I said earlier that all of us have banded together for the benefit of these children, and we are all suffering over the loss of Victor.

This type of pain is something that I would not wish on any parent. I have been homeless, beaten and raped, but to combine them all doesn't compare to the anguish of laying your child to rest. Some say to me that Victor was not technically my child, so why do I grieve so. And to all of those self-centered idiots I will tell you this plain simple truth. YOU DO NOT HAVE TO GIVE BIRTH TO A CHILD FOR THAT CHILD TO BE YOUR CHILD! Victor was not technically my son, but you couldn't tell that to him or me.

I loved him as if he were mine, and he was. Technically, he wasn't birthed from any of us. He is Deuce's little brother that she took in when he was three years old because their mother passed away on June 2nd 1992. She was very sick and asked Deuce to care for him days before she died. Deuce was only twenty at the time, and she was married to her first husband. This was a young couple with a one year-old baby (#2), and she was about to give birth to her son (#3).

They gladly took on the extra responsibility. Next thing they knew, Mom died, and Deuce gave birth to #3 three days later. Imagine the emotional shift that they were going through, planning a funeral for her mother and celebrating the birth of a son while tending to a toddler daughter (#2) and taking care of Deuce's baby brother (#1). Things were hard for Deuce and her first husband, but they progressed until they divorced. As I said earlier, now we are all partners, and we do not allow egos and drama to destroy what we have with our children.

We all had to strive to set good examples for the kids, and I can rest easy knowing that Victor started to "GET IT" before he passed away. I came into Victor's life when he was still very young. I had the pleasure of watching him transform from a little boy who was afraid of his own shadow at times to becoming a strong man of principle and ethics. When my father died in 2007, Victor proudly stood in front of that church and spoke from the podium saying that he was my son and that he was especially proud of my strength as I dealt with the death of my dad. There was maturity and power in his voice as he spoke and commanded the attention of the entire congregation.

Victor displayed strength in so many ways. You know your child was a good person when you hear reports of his strength and leadership from people whom you don't know but who knew him. This is especially insightful to parents because we never really know what kind of job we did rearing our children until we see the fruits of those labors. All we heard from a multitude of people was of his exemplary character and his passion to help others. He had a natural zeal to improve the lives of everybody around him in one way or another. Our son listened to his parents and has honored us all.

I know that there are a lot of parents who are dealing with the loss of a child. Parents of soldiers, police officers, fire fighters, public servants and even school-age children are dealing with this pain. We all remember the Oklahoma City bombings, 911, the Columbine High School tragedy along with a multitude of fatal shootings at college campuses.

Our children are also being snatched away from us in record numbers during times of war and gang violence. No one will ever understand the amount of pain that you struggle with. You, unfortunately, have to deal with this ugly issue. What helped me deal with my pain is when I reached out to others who have dealt with it before me, and I help those brave parents who are dealing with it along side of me.

The time after the funeral can be both stressful and unpredictable. You try to function and continue with your life, but you will be on an emotional rollercoaster for a while. One moment you're laughing with friends over good times with your child, and the next you can't stop crying. No one can console you at those moments. You have to just let it go and deal with each emotion as it comes. You have to ride out the shock of the situation, survive the gut-wrenching pain that there is nothing you can do to bring your child back, then deal with the fact that you are extremely angry over it; you must face the confusion as to why it had to happen to your child, find plenty of support during the time of sadness, which can lead to severe depression, and finally overcome the tremendous amount of guilt that you may feel afterwards.

This is going to be the most difficult thing that you may ever face in life but please know that eventually it will get better. What helped me are my own spiritual beliefs. I know that my son will never suffer again, and he is in a much better place than this chaotic world. I believe that we are all energy, and energy never dies, but it evolves and transforms. I believe that my son is still with me spiritually, and I will never let him go.

My family and I will keep him alive through our love for him and by helping others who are dealing with this awful experience. I know these words may not be helping much now, but please know that I have gone through this and eventually the pain eases. It never goes away, but it does become manageable eventually.

Everybody responds to these types of tragedies differently. You may have to postpone your grief in order to support your loved ones. I had to somehow hold on to my feelings as I tended to my wife and six other children. We responded in different ways. Deuce and my daughters cried openly while my sons tried to be strong and just hide their pain.

Men are taught to never cry or show emotion because it is seen as a form of weakness. I never told my boys to be that way, but it is something that society and peer pressure bring about. I held my sons and told them that it was okay to let it out. I eventually let go of my own pain and cried in front of them; I told them that it takes a real man to show emotion, and there was nothing wrong with crying over their brother. They finally let it go, and we progressed slowly day by day.

Life was challenging as some of our basic perceptions changed after Victor's death. I was driving large tanker trucks over the road, and my cargo consisted of highly flammable liquids and poisonous gasses. I was only home five days a month, and Deuce wanted me home more. She was a former over-the-road truck driver and hated being away from home for so long. It made sense to me because I was missing precious time with my children while chasing a dollar. All of the money in the world cannot buy back time. Something told me to come home for awhile, and I'm glad I did.

I would have felt nothing but guilt if I had been on the road when Victor died. I would not have been there to hold my wife and children and ultimately be the support that my family needed. My place was there and not on the road. I decided that life is too short. There had to be something that I could do to support my family while spending as much time as I could with them. I quit my job and found something local so I could be home every day. No job is worth losing time with your family because you never know when tragedy may happen.

This was a hard time for me because I had to mourn, but the bills were still coming in. The threat of financial loss is a very real one. I didn't feel like working or doing anything for that matter. All I wanted to do was hold on tight to Deuce and the kids, but I had to push through and make sure our basic needs were being met. This can be a difficult thing for you as well. The only thing that is important is that there is a roof over your family's head and food for them to eat. Everything else is pushed to the back burner for now. If possible, call all of your bill collectors and tell them what is going on. Some may give you thirty days to recoup, and some may not. I made the calls and some actually told me to take my time dealing with my loss and to call them when I could make a payment.

The most important thing I want to convey is that even though the situation is insane; do not let it drive you crazy. Do all the crying you can, get all the support you need, and find it in you to fight deep down within your soul to maintain your sanity. You will be tempted to just give up, but you can't. You are still alive, and you must live on for your child no matter how difficult it is right now. Be careful to fight off depression and other health issues that can develop from the tremendous stress you are under.

The thing that helped me the most was to write through my pain and express my feelings no matter what they were. I kept a journal and always referred back to my good days when I was having a bad day. My good days consisted of writing about happy memories and time well spent with Victor. Sometimes just a small hint of a smile can break through a large amount of sadness and despair.

It may take some time before things have some semblance of normalcy. No amount of time or money can bring your baby back, but after some healing, think about your child's legacy. What do you want your baby to be remembered for? My son left this world due to his vehicle not having the proper safety equipment. If his vehicle had been pulled from service and the proper equipment had been installed, there is a very strong chance that my boy would still be here. I decided it was important to create a positive legacy from my son's preventable death; therefore, I am in the process of creating the Victor Sims Foundation to be a charity and a memorial to my son to raise money specifically for families who are suffering the loss of a child.

Hopefully, many lives will be changed because of the foundation's efforts, and we trust that our work will continue to show the world how special Victor was by creating a strong legacy in his name. As long as I live, I will push this agenda so my son and others like him will never be swept under the rug and forgotten! I took the time to write down my thoughts about my son before the funeral. You may read them if you like.

A Valiant Soul

Let me tell you about a man of small stature but tremendous character. He was a man with the heart and tenacity of a lion but who was filled with so much love that he could be an example to everyone around him. The man I speak about is my son Victor. The reason why I can say these things is because I watched him grow and mature into a person whom I can honestly say that I respected.

It is hard to see your child grow up and deal with those tough issues that life can bring (girls, peer-pressure and so on), but it is equally rewarding to see him shine through adversity and never give up. He had a growing concern about being compared to thugs because of his long hair. My son would say, *"I want people to see that a black man can have long hair and not be the stereotypical trouble maker. I am a strong man with character and goals. I am different, and I will prove them wrong!"*

He would sit me down and tell me what his plans were, and I would use reverse psychology and tell him that he would fail. I was always happy to see him prove me wrong, and he did it very often and was not shy about reminding me of it! I have had the privilege of watching a little boy filled with excuses about why he couldn't do certain things blossom into a strong figure who gave no excuses but simply provided answers and results. It is not easy to lead and have the daunting task of being the man of the house when dad is away while being responsible for all of the mischief of six younger siblings. It is the truly valiant soul who will volunteer or sacrifice himself to be disciplined for the good of the group in order for no one else to get in trouble.

This is the mark of a leader...this is the nature of a champion... this is my son! He was, and still is, a shining example to his peers, co-workers and everyone who was blessed to have him in their lives. So I cry out to the heavens to my son Victor. It was an honor and a privilege to help raise you and watch you grow up to become a fine, upstanding man of exemplary character. You are loved and terribly missed, and I promise that I will fight so everyone knows the awesome man that you had become!

Love always from your dad

That is my personal letter to my son, and I am sure that if you are dealing with this kind of tragedy, you have some special words of your own for your child. Keep your head up and fight through the pain and establish a strong legacy, so we all know how special your child was and how much you love him or her. God Bless You.

20 Q'S & A'S

IF YOU HAVE A question or concern that I did not get into throughout
the book, I hope this section will help you. These are the twenty most
frequently asked questions I get whenever I do speaking engagements
or get off my e-mail.

Q. *My ex is a bitch! What do I do with a woman who will not accept my
    change?*

A. Lots of men have come to me over the years and said that all of this
    mumbo-jumbo with your ex-wives might have worked for you, but
    my ex is a real bitch! The first thing you need to do is to stop refer-
    ring to her as a bitch, even if she acts like one! Unfortunately, there
    may be times when it is best to cut all ties and leave the communica-
    tion to a minimum. This is what I had to do in the beginning, but
    there are those people who maybe we just were not meant to get
    along with! You had sex, and that's all it was, but you had a baby in
    the process. I encourage you to keep trying. After the wave of emo-

135

tions has passed over time, most people generally let their guard down a little and are willing to listen.

Q. *My ex and her family constantly bad mouth me to my kids. They are trying to turn my kids against me! What do I do?*

A. One very important thing to remember is that this is about your child or children and not about you. This whole process is not designed to be easy for you or your ex. It is meant for your children to be able to adjust to the broken relationship and not experience a war of their parents in which they have to choose whom they love the most, mom or dad. Children should never have to choose sides between two feuding parents and their families. All the back biting needs to end. Do not insult or talk badly about your ex in front of your children, no matter what she is doing! Keep SHOWING your kids that you love them by spending as much time with them as possible, proving that you are not that horrible monster they say you are! Children are very smart, and eventually they see who the real monsters are. ***The more negativity a person pumps into a child, the more that child will later resent them!*** You need to instruct your family to follow your example as well, and let her family drink all the "HATER-AID"!

Q. *I hate myself for the negative things that I did in the relationship and hurting my family. How do I forgive myself?*

A. The very first thing you need to do after a major breakup is to forgive yourself for anything that you may have contributed to the relationship ending. This is so vitally important, and most people miss this. Here's a life lesson for you...No one is perfect! You and everybody around you know that you screwed up, but it's not the end of the world. I hope you remember one of my parables: *"As long as I am alive, I have a chance."* You can fix whatever is broken in time, but you must first fix yourself by forgiving yourself. Love yourself enough to forgive, and get on with the business of healing. *People normally treat you as you treat yourself.* Hating yourself will bring nothing but more hatred towards you!

Q.   *I am so disappointed with myself for being with a person who manipulated me for so long. I wonder if I'm worthy of having someone good in my life. How do I get over my ex and find love again?*

A.   The quick fix for most guys is to sleep with as many women as they can in a short period of time, hoping to forget about their exes. This sounds good, but there can be nothing more detrimental to your recovery. You may be experiencing pleasure for the moment, but you are trying to use a band-aid for a bullet wound. We as men have been taught to cover up our feelings and "just deal with it like a man" since we were kids. Going down this slippery slope will do nothing but further cloud our judgment and possibly put us in the position of being a dad of several of those "throw away kids" I mentioned earlier! Now here we go again with the same vicious cycle perpetuating itself because we keep doing the same thing expecting different results! Can I say insanity?

Let me give you a few suggestions to help. Hit the gym, work out that aggression, and get yourself healthy. Concentrate on taking care of you instead of being mad at her. You need to start getting plenty of rest and start eating the right foods. Stay busy by picking up good habits or finally taking on that project or life experience that you always wanted to do but didn't have enough time for. There is always a place that you've always longed to see and something you've always wanted to do. Take a timeout and concentrate on your happiness outside of women for awhile, and get back in the game when you're ready! Getting yourself right will lead you to the right woman this time! By knowing yourself, you will know what you want and need from her and not get screwed!

Q.   *Now that I am a single dad, what are some great activities I can do with my kids?*

A.   I found it incredibly fun when I took my kids to the park and just played football and threw a Frisbee around. Another great activity is to rent or buy a tandem bicycle. These bikes have a seat for everybody and are wonderful on those beautiful warm afternoons for you and your kids to tear up the sidewalk!

Q.   *I have a new girlfriend. When is it a good time to introduce her to my kids?*

A.   This is a very good question. The fact that she is willing to be your girlfriend knowing that you are a single parent is a good thing. I typically tell guys to hold their horses and really get to know this woman before you introduce her to your babies. Figure out what she really means to you first. If she is someone that you just have frequent sexual relations with, do not introduce her to your kids! You have no intention of keeping her around. If you get a good vibe from her, "The Kid Subject" has come up, and you really want her to stick around and get serious, then a few months is plausible. Eight weeks of spending time with someone is ample time to see through to who they really are. I generally take longer to scope her out. It's up to you, but be careful! The last thing you need is a psycho woman around your kids and your ex screaming to the courts, "I told you so!"

Q.   *Where can I find a family friendly woman?*

A.   Now that you are a single dad, your taste in women has hopefully changed for the better. Stay away from the clubs and bars! I am not saying that all club and bar chicks are bad, but c'mon, let's be real! These are not the type of women whom you screw within a few hours of knowing them, and then introduce them to your kids as their new mommy! It's time to upgrade and look in different places for that jewel who is out there waiting for you. Go to sporting events or just find women at the events where you take your kids. Good family friendly environments are excellent places to find a good woman. These women are probably single parents as well looking for a great guy like you to walk into their lives!

Q.   *I've been single for so long that I think I might have lost my edge when it comes to sex. Can you give me some pointers?*

A.   I love questions like this! I'm going to break this down in sections because this is a subject that I just can't skimp over, so let's get right to it!

1.   Find and get to know the clitoris! All those myths that "A real man doesn't go down on a woman" will leave you alone and hard for the rest of your days! The last thing you want is to be a single dad in bed. You want to be that monster that she raves to her friends about and loses sleep over because she

can't get you out of her head! Let your fingers do the walking to stroke her as you lick her frequently. Suck on it until she pops! A useful technique is to spell out her name with your tongue as you whisper the letter before you simulate it! Bringing pleasure to a woman will make her stick around!

2. Let her be in charge! Women like to be in charge sometimes when they want to be in control of achieving an orgasm. This can best be done with her on top in the "Cow Girl" position. Let her straddle you and ride you for awhile. Let her fingers dig into your chest as she leans back; now it's time for you to make your move. Pull her closer to you so her torso is close to yours. Tell her to arch her back keeping her crotch on the base of your penis as she moves from side to side, up and down! To maximize this technique, rise up a little and hug her close as she rides you. She will be a very happy woman when it is over!

Q. *I want to be known for something besides being my kid's dad. How do I get myself out there and become a success?*

A. You need what many people call a professional name. Take my name for instance. Yahanseh (ya-hawn-say) is my real name, and it is a marketable name because it is unique. There are not too many people named Yahanseh in this country, so nine times out of ten when you hear that name it's probably me. I love that! Where do you know Yahanseh from? He's the guy who wrote that book about his seven kids and two ex-wives and talks about conquering adversity in all its ugly forms and personal responsibility. The fact that I wrote this book makes me a credible resource for some to find answers they seek.

Most people are not comfortable using their real name. As a matter of fact, most authors and entertainers choose pen names or stage names to protect themselves from unscrupulous characters. I learned that little lesson the hard way. I remember being visited by a crazy female fan at my door step! She simply looked me up in the phone book and knocked at my door! She was mentally unstable and ranted about how we belong together and that she was not taking no for an answer! I called the police, installed an advanced home security system, and I have not heard from her in years. I hope to never see her again!

I also have a pen name "NYGHTSTORM" when I am writing my dark fiction novels and screenplays. It's like becoming another person as I express myself differently because of a litany of controversial subjects that I explore. Letting your stronger, bolder, more confident side out and giving it a name is nothing new. Beyonce Knowles becomes "Sasha Fierce," a stronger side of herself, when she is performing. You must become "Mr. Somebody," a man who is confident, knows what he is talking about, and who does not share your insecurities.

Become the go-to guy at work, or write a book dealing with issues that you are an expert on. Practice public speaking and getting comfortable being around large groups of people. Kick your shyness to the curb and assertively go after your dream! Become the commodity or product that people will be willing to spend their hard-earned money on, and have a name that everybody will learn to know and trust!

Q. *I'm a "good man"; how come i can't get the sexy women?*

A. This question has been presented to me a few times. Unfortunately, most women are attracted to the bad guy. These guys are fun, exciting, unpredictable and full of mystery. This has perplexed me as well because like I said earlier, I have been on both sides. I was nearly destroyed emotionally by women as the good guy and worshiped as a Nubian god when I was a dog! But I will say that the rise of the "Good Man" is here! Women are getting tired of being beaten and cheated on by the bad boys. They are looking for that happy medium. They don't want a boy scout, but they don't want a felon. They want a nice guy with an edge. So come out of your introverted shell and become the nice family man that can kick some ass if need be, and be the knight in shining armor that rides a Harley in gangster leather!

Q. *My kids hate my new girlfriend. What do I do?*

A. Children need time to readjust to the fact that their parents are no longer together. They may not like anybody that you bring around for awhile. First, ask your kids why they do not like her! Is she acting differently around them when you are not around? Is she doing something to them that you are not aware of? This is very important, and you need to know why they hate her. If she is abusing your kids in any way, then a sit down talk with her and your children is needed immediately! Speak with her in front of your children, and bring up the accusations against her. This will bring out the truth.

It will show you if she is really doing those things or if your kids are just trying to get rid of her. If she is hurting or mistreating them, kick her to the curb and call the police if necessary. Never put your own carnal desires above the needs of your children.

If she is not the "Demon Woman" they say she is, your kids could be acting out because they are unhappy with the divorce. There are things you can do to warm them up to your new sweetie if she turns out to be okay. When I finally found someone whom I wanted to have a serious relationship with, I had to gradually include her in our activities. I first sat my children down and spoke to them about how much I loved them. I told them I would always love their mother regardless of the divorce. I asked them if they wanted me to be happy, and they naturally said yes. I told them that I had met someone special who made me happy, but I wanted to include them in my decision making as far as seeing her further. This made them feel important and included in my life. They felt that their opinion mattered to me.

After the talk, I took everyone to the park, including my new girlfriend. They hit it off, and they saw how happy she made me. She also told them that she knew how important they were to me and that she could never replace their mother. She also said that she was here to help, not hurt. This was very important! Your new girlfriend has to do her part also if she wants to truly be a positive part of your lives.

Q. *I have a drinking problem, and I sometimes lash out at my kids. How can I stop?*

A.   Alcoholism is a disease that needs to be treated immediately! If you cannot stop on your own, please seek professional help. I urge anyone with an unhealthy addiction to fight as hard as you can to get clean! If you do not seek help, you may end up doing something that you will regret while you're intoxicated! YOU and your family are too important to leave this matter unresolved! Have your children stay with a loved one until you get the help you need. This will protect them and give you the time you need to heal.

Q.   *A friend of my daughter is being molested by her step-dad. What do I do?*

A.   Call the cops! If you are sure that she is being molested, do not hesitate! If you are unsure, speak with her and your daughter, and have a discussion dealing with the issue. This is a very touchy subject, but it should never be ignored. When in doubt, call the authorities and let them sort it out. That little girl may be screaming for help, but no one is listening!

Q.   *My son's girlfriend is coming on to me. What do I do?*

A.   This could be just a crush, and most teen-age crushes go away. But if she is really coming on to you and trying to heat things up, first talk to your son, and tell him about the advances. Your son will quickly deal with the situation himself. It is never a good idea to entertain advances from someone who is supposed to be in a relationship with your child. If all else fails, tell your son that she is not welcome in your house because of her advances toward you.

Q.   *My daughter just had her first period and her mother is no where around. What do I do?*

A. These things can be very embarrassing to her, and you may have to approach her in a very sensitive and understanding way. If there are any female relatives around, ask them for their assistance. If not, then you are on your own! Tell her this is the natural cycle of her development and that she is blossoming into a young lady. Reassure her that she is not a freak and every woman has to go through this. Give her your support by telling her that you are there for her, and get used to shopping in the feminine aisle!

Q. *My daughter is pregnant and wants to get an abortion. I feel that abortion is a sin and against my church teachings. What do I do?*

A. I never get involved in a person's beliefs regarding politics or religion. These are principles that people live and even die for. Talk to your daughter and give her other options. Ask yourself, are you willing to help her with this baby and not judge or condemn her? Most young ladies seek abortion because they are afraid of the damnation from their loved ones. I told you earlier in the book about a young lady who killed herself because her father was a preacher, and she knew what he would think about her. Please learn from that lesson, and be willing to be open and responsive to her needs. I know you love your child, but you must remember that the ultimate decision belongs to her. She needs your love and support regardless of her decision.

Q. *I found out that my son is gay. How do I have a relationship with him when I oppose his lifestyle?*

A. The last thing you need to do is bring a ton of girls around him to get back his "manhood." A friend of mine bought his son eight full-feature porn flicks to get his son to like girls again. The plan backfired because his son was watching the guys instead of the girls! These things are touchy and can be very difficult to deal with as a parent. He may be going through a phase of experimenting and trying to find himself. The only thing you can do is to continue to love him for whom he is. You cannot force him to stop being gay. As a matter of fact, if you push too hard, you will push him further away from you! So, decide what's important here -- your relationship with your son or your pride as a dad. We can try as hard as we can to mold our children into whom we want them to be, but they will ultimately become whom they want to be!

Q. *My son is a teenage criminal and refuses to change. How do I support him without supporting his crimes?*

A. Your son needs to spend some time in jail, and hopefully that will wake him up! But before it gets to that point, put him in a "Scared Straight Program" with your local law enforcement agency. They take kids up to sixteen years of age. It worked for my son! A healthy dose of reality should shake him up a bit. Some of these kids commit crimes because they know they will only get a slap on the wrist because they are minors! I know the system is screwed up, but you as the parent must take the appropriate action. Do not baby him, and let him know that what he is doing is unacceptable!

Q. *I found out that my children are calling my ex-wife's boyfriend daddy; they are not married, so he is not even their stepfather. I don't want to hurt or confuse the kids, but I don't like it. How do I handle this?*

A. I know that this could be a crushing blow to any man. My stepchildren called me by my middle name for years. They call me "Pop" every now and then because of how I treat them. I love them as my own and support them. They knew that I was not their dad, but they gave me respect as their second dad because of my love for them. Evaluate and see how this boyfriend of your ex-wife is treating them. If he is loving them as his own and being the "Second Daddy," then you know that he is being good to your kids. Express your concern to your ex-wife, and ask her if she plans on having a future with this man. She may tell you to butt out and that it's none of your business, but it is a subject that needs to be addressed. The welfare of your children is the most important thing. If he is being good to them, then let him be. Please remember he can never replace you, and you are still "The Man." However, it hurts to know that you have no power in your ex-wife's home unless there is something bad going on. Talk to your kids and tell them how you feel, and continue to be the great "Real Daddy" that you are for them. They will always be your children, no matter who comes and goes in your ex-wife's life.

Q. *My children are telling me that their mom's boyfriend is beating her even with them around, and sometime they jump in to help. I personally have been so hurt by her that a part of me feels she is getting what she deserves, but my kids are being traumatized. She is a great mom, even if her relationship skills with men suck, and I know if I take the children, she would be devastated, but I can't stand what this is doing to them. What should I do?*

A. Family violence is never an easy subject to address. Pair this with your feelings that she is getting what she deserves because of how she treated you, and it really becomes complicated. There is a sadistic nature in all of us when we experience joy because of the hardship or pain of someone who has hurt us. The fact that he is beating her is not a healthy environment for your kids. They are even jumping in to get him off of your ex-wife when he is beating her, which can be extremely dangerous for them. You may need to intervene and get a court order to remove them from the house until she can get her life together. I hate to bring in the courts, but this may be your only option at this time if she is not willing to let you get them temporarily. It will devastate her, but it will also force her to make some very hard decisions for her well-being as well as for the kids. The safety of the children is the most important thing!

THANK YOU FOR READING my book and I hope that it has been helpful to you. It has been very therapeutic for me to finally get all this stuff off my chest. I know that you have what it takes to be a success in parenting and in life. I hope that all the women that read this gets a better understanding about men and the way we respond to you. My goal is to help heal open wounds and to ultimately help people to help themselves to the lives they deserve. We all want to be happy and loved and I hope this book helped you to free yourself from your own psychological prison. Everyone has a story in them that can help someone else. I know this because you have read my story and I look forward to reading yours! GO OUT AND HAVE A GREAT LIFE!!!!

Sincerely,
Y. G. NYGHTSTORM

THIS BOOK IS ALSO dedicated to Deuce, My second wife and the love of my life. It doesn't matter if we are married, divorced, and married again; you will always have my love and respect. Thank you for memorizing every lyric from every song I wrote from a failed music career; and thank you for reading every word from every novel I have written. Some of my work may never see the light of day but you always told me that I was a best selling author even if I didn't believe it myself. You believed in me when others didn't and you are truly a special, once in a lifetime woman that I will always cherish and never forget. Thank you for being my girl when we're together and my best friend when we are not.

SPECIAL THANKS

1. Uno "THE FIRST WOMAN I EVER LOVED"
2. Dr. Alduan Tartt "THE LOVE DOCTOR"
3. Dr. Val Dodson "THE EDITOR EXTRODINAIRE"
4. Dexter Vines "THE COMIC BOOK GENIUS"
5. Rico Robinson "THE WISE PHYLOSOPHER"
6. Carlos Jackson "THE FRIEND THAT GOT ME THROUGH"
7. Bryant Rayford "THE ONE MAN SHOW"
8. Dr. John Thomas "THE CHIROPRACTER FROM HEAVEN"

PARABLES FOR A BETTER LIFE

1. "As a father, there will be times when you must take full responsibility and sometimes take matters within your own hands to fix them."

2. "Where there's smoke, there's fire. Be prepared to put it out!"

3. "Change the things that I can change; everything else is dead."

4. "When there is no direction or purpose chaos will lead and destruction follows."

5. "Children follow the lead of their fathers so where are you leading them?"

6. "Do not destroy your life over someone who will not live for you."

7. "...what goes around comes around. You never have to punish anyone because the universe will do it for you."

8. "...to get your kids attention you first have to listen..."

9. "...true leadership precedes results."

10. "If you need something in your life, provide that need for someone else first."

11. "You have the power because you are the dad!"

12. "...regardless if I feel that someone is wrong, I need to make the proper decision that will lead to a positive conclusion."

13. "Sometimes we need to look in the mirror to see where our problems lie."

14. "A man can change himself for the greater good if he so desires to do so."

15. "You should never allow your children to hold you hostage in your own home!"

16. "Never involve the cops in domestic issues if you can help it!"

17. "...as long as I'm alive, I still have a chance."

18. "There is unlimited power that fathers have when they are operating and conducting themselves the right way."

19. "We must not live our lives in secrets and negativity because when the time comes, our children may tell the ugly truth about us after we are dead!"

20. "Whatever you are accustomed to is what you will desire psychologically."

21. "You can fail a million times, but just succeed once and your life will change forever!"

22. "The more negativity a person pumps into a child, the more that child will later resent them!"

23. "People normally treat you as you treat yourself."

24. "Education is the STRONGEST weapon."

25. "Pleasure cost in pain dollars and it is very expensive. Are you willing to write the check?"

26. "A man has all the friends and women in the world when he has something that they want! As soon as a man's status drops, he crashes and burns, his entourage will disappear as fast as it came!"

27. "Independence is freedom and it is contagious to all of those that seek it!"

28. "The function of great power and great wisdom is to do good."

29. "Together we stand...we shall never fall!"

www.ingramcontent.com/pod-product-compliance
Lightning Source LLC
Chambersburg PA
CBHW020427290526
45785CB00002B/728